OXFORD
INDIA SHORT
INTRODUCTIONS

# AFFIRMATIVE ACTION
# IN INDIA

The Oxford India Short
Introductions are concise,
stimulating, and accessible guides
to different aspects of India.
Combining authoritative analysis,
new ideas, and diverse perspectives,
they discuss subjects which are
topical yet enduring, as also
emerging areas of study and debate.

OXFORD
INDIA SHORT
INTRODUCTIONS

# AFFIRMATIVE
# ACTION IN
# INDIA

ASHWINI DESHPANDE

**OXFORD**
UNIVERSITY PRESS

OXFORD
UNIVERSITY PRESS

Oxford University Press is a department of the University of Oxford.
It furthers the University's objective of excellence in research, scholarship,
and education by publishing worldwide. Oxford is a registered trademark of
Oxford University Press in the UK and in certain other countries

Published in India by
Oxford University Press
22 Workspace, 2nd Floor, 1/22 Asaf Ali Road, New Delhi 110002, India

First Edition published in 2013

**15th impression 2025**

ISBN-13: 978-0-19-809208-7
ISBN-10: 0-19-809208-3

Typeset in 11/15.6 Bembo Std
by Excellent Laser Typesetters, Pitampura, Delhi 110 034
**Printed in India by Manipal Technologies Limited, Manipal**

*For Ketaki,*
*with the hope that she might, one day,*
*see a world where affirmative action is superfluous*

# Contents

# Contents

# Preface

As I was working on the last chapter of *The Grammar of Caste: Economic Discrimination in Contemporary India* (2011) which deals with affirmative action (AA), it was clear to me that the chapter should have appropriately been a book. In order to keep the length of that chapter in sync with the rest of the book, I focused on a few new studies, rather than making a futile attempt to be comprehensive in that short space. Also, after Marc Galanter's comprehensive, balanced, and nuanced study of India's caste-based affirmative action programme, *Competing Equalities* (1984), not too many studies can hope to surpass that level of detail and expert knowledge, and effortlessly straddle the worlds of social science and law. I agreed to Oxford University Press' offer to write this short introduction for two reasons. One, given that I wanted to elaborate further on the question of affirmative action, this was the perfect opportunity, coming as it did on the heels of *Grammar*. Two, the *Oxford India Short Introduction* series has a clear mandate in terms of a short and focused exposition of a given subject, so there is no compulsion for me to match the depth and breadth of other important scholarly works on the topic, of which there are plenty in circulation, in addition to Galanter's excellent work. This is aimed at a general audience, not only those with a background in social science, and it provides the rationale, details, and an assessment of the AA programme in India. It summarizes the important results of the vast body of research on this subject and provides leads for further reading to those interested in pursuing specific aspects of the issue.

I would like to thank Thomas E. Weisskopf, Dean Spears, Bhaskar Dutta, and an anonymous referee from OUP for useful comments on an earlier draft, while taking full responsibility for all remaining gaps. Since these issues are part of my ongoing research, I hope to be able to address the remaining lacunae in my subsequent work.

ASHWINI DESHPANDE
December 2012                                New Delhi

# 1

# The Rationale for
# Affirmative Action

In 1990, large parts of the country, particularly north India, were thrown in turmoil. The central government had announced the implementation of the Mandal Commission Report, which extended quotas from the pre-existing 22.5 per cent for Scheduled Castes and Tribes (SCs and STs) by another 27 per cent for 'Other Backward Classes' (OBCs), and thousands of students were on the streets for weeks demanding a reversal of this apparently retrograde move. As one commentator put it: 'Brilliant minds, young, eager and keen to make a mark in the world, if pushed to a corner by apparent injustice can only spark off one thing—rebellion.' As the agitation gathered strength, it was widely supported by the mainstream media, and sparked off a massive debate on a set of questions raised by the agitating students: 'Why should an essentially divisive element and a carry-over of the traditional society be a factor in determining something as modern as jobs? Why should people be divided on the basis of surnames? And why, oh why, should merit be not the first, foremost, and the only factor in determining who stood first in the job race?' Pertinent questions indeed, and worthy of serious attention from every citizen of modern India.

Interestingly, these same students who were asking very germane questions about why (something as modern as) occupation should be linked to (an antiquated system such as) caste did not see the irony in their mode of protest. Protesting students (and their parents) sat on the streets of Connaught Place in New Delhi, some shining shoes, others with brooms in their hands sweeping the streets, some even going around with begging bowls, with associated slogans suggesting this is what *they* would be reduced to doing, if additional quotas in higher education were introduced. This was accompanied by a widespread lampooning of Prime Minister V.P. Singh for having introduced the demon of reservations: one evocative cartoon showed him in a ship with three flags—SC, ST, and OBC—and with some people, presumably belonging to these groups happy in the ship, while other students, presumably upper castes, all around the ship were sinking in the sea with degrees in their hands. While the debate was sparked off by an extension of reservations to OBCs, impassioned pleas were made not only for a reversal of the recently introduced reservations, but of all quotas. For instance, the Class I employees association, which at the time had only about 6 per cent reserved category officers (and thus was overwhelmingly non-reserved), demanded a roll-back of all reservations, claiming that quotas were adversely affecting efficiency of administration.

The protestors and their supporters did not see any incongruity between the central question they were asking—about why caste should matter in job markets—and their pejorative portrayal of certain traditional caste occupations. Clearly, the implication was that all was well with a world in which these occupations were performed by 'them' and not by 'us'. Colleges, universities, and prestigious jobs, should rightfully belong to 'us', while sweeping, cleaning, and mending shoes are 'their' jobs. Ironically, the status quo was not seen as casteist or ridden with caste divisions, but the proposed remedy was widely criticized as *introducing* caste divisions. To be fair, there was a section among the opponents to quotas, who recognized the problem of caste divisions, but argued that this particular remedy was ill-suited.

If the protestors had read the writings of Bhim Rao Ambedkar, the chief architect of the Indian Constitution, who was instrumental in making preferential policies a part of the constitutional mandate, they would have been struck by the overlap in the questions they were asking and the questions that Ambedkar raised, sharply and eloquently, through his writings, speeches, and actions. He believed, for instance, that the caste system was not a benign division of labour, but a 'division of labourers'. Additionally, he argued, it is a 'hierarchy in which the division of labourers are graded one above the other'. This division is 'not spontaneous, it is not based on natural aptitudes ... [the caste system] is an attempt to assign tasks to individuals in advance, *selected not on the basis of trained original capacities, but on that of the social status of the parents ... this stratification of occupations which is the result of the caste system* is positively pernicious' (Ambedkar 1936, emphasis added).

A juxtaposition of Ambedkar's characterization of the occupational division produced by the caste system and the protestors' belief that caste quotas will produce hierarchies and divisions, based not on merit but birth, should compel us to think hard about cause and effect: are quotas promoting caste divisions or redressing them? The protestors were mourning the death of 'merit' due to the introduction of quotas; Ambedkar, and others before him, had pointed out how precisely the existence of the caste system did not recognize individual merit, but assigned jobs by birth into one caste or another. By this logic, quotas were not killing merit, the caste system was.

This was not the first time that this debate had taken place in India. Indeed, such debates, which are extremely contentious, have erupted with ferocity all over the world where affirmative action (AA) measures have been introduced in favour of disadvantaged groups. This volume discusses the 'why' and 'how' of AA with glimpses into the history of the programme and offers some perspective on where India stands today both in terms of group disparities as well as in terms of proposed remedies.

## India's AA Programme

India's AA programme, which should be viewed as a compensatory discrimination measure, is primarily caste-based, although there is some AA for women in the electoral sphere. The term 'affirmative action' is of relatively recent origin—the term was first used in 1961 in the United States by John F. Kennedy in the context of policies designed to promote equal opportunity or non-discrimination. I use the term 'quotas/reservations' and 'AA' interchangeably in this book, while recognizing that AA is a broader concept than quotas. The quota or reservation policy in India, which is the core of AA, is essentially a policy of preferential treatment for certain disadvantaged groups. AA in India, as elsewhere in the world, is contentious for three reasons. One, there is considerable debate over the assessment of caste disparities, the prima facie reason for the existence of AA—whether these are significant at all; if yes, to what extent and in which sphere; and whether they have been narrowing over time. Two, there is a larger debate about whether caste is the valid indicator of backwardness or should AA be defined in terms of class/income or other social markers such as religion. Three, there is the overarching debate about whether AA is desirable at all, in any form, either through quotas or preferential boosts, regardless of which social identity is used as its anchor. This *Short Introduction* not only provides factual details, the nuts-and-bolts of AA, but also sketches out the larger picture, with further leads on specific aspects for the interested reader.

In the polarized debate around AA, it is either demonized as the root of all evil or valorized as the panacea for eliminating discrimination. It is worth noting at the outset that Ambedkar himself did not see reservations or AA as a panacea. He did not believe that the caste system could be made less malignant. He said '... my ideal would be a society based on *Liberty, Equality and Fraternity* ... [the caste system] means a state of slavery ... a society in which some men are forced to accept from others the purposes which control their conduct' (Ambedkar 1936, emphasis in original). He was constantly engaged with the question of strategies and instruments which would lead to the annihilation of caste altogether. We examine the details of the evolution of the reservation system in the next chapter. For now, it might be useful to start with a brief statement on what AA policies are designed to achieve. The following opening remarks are about AA policies in general (regardless of the instrument used, for example, quotas or preferences); the discussion gets more nuanced and fleshed out as we proceed.

## The Purpose and Scope of AA

Broadly speaking, AA consists of a set of anti-discrimination measures intended to provide access to preferred positions in a society for members of groups that would otherwise be excluded or under-represented. It provides a mechanism to address contemporary exclusion, particularly a mechanism to de-segregate elites. Even though AA primarily addresses contemporary exclusion, we should be fully aware that historical factors such as the history of slavery in the US or that of caste-based discrimination in India have been instrumental in making AA politically feasible in the two countries and that there are similar historical factors relevant in other countries pursuing AA. Affirmative action can be, and has been, utilized in different parts of the world to change the social composition of elite position holders, making those positions more representative of the caste/ethnic/gender composition of the society as a whole (Zweigenhaft and Domhoff 1998). AA is not a conventional redistributive measure, in the sense that it does not lead to a redistribution of wealth or assets in the same way that, say a policy of land reforms, would achieve. It simply alters the composition of elite positions in society.

It is not meant to be an anti-poverty measure, nor an employment *generation* measure. It should be noted that class-based government programmes, such as anti-poverty or employment-generation programmes, designed to ameliorate poverty or provide livelihood support, could also reflect underlying social biases, in that deserving members of stigmatized groups could get disproportionately excluded from such programmes. The rationale for AA is that given systematic and multifaceted discrimination against certain groups, the normal process of development might not automatically close the gaps between the marginalized and dominant groups because dominant groups will disproportionately corner the fruits of development. While it is true that the lives of large sections of marginalized groups might not be touched by AA given

9

its targeting of elite positions, AA nevertheless fulfils an important function by providing some members of the disadvantaged communities a voice in decision-making; by placing them in prestigious jobs and elite educational institutions, it provides the community with say.

Since caste disparities and caste-based discrimination have been the chief *raison d'etre* of the Indian AA programme, I start with a short background of the caste system in India to set the stage which has seen extremely heated, often violent, debates on AA.

## Caste in India: Some Definitions and Enumeration Issues

As is well known, the caste system in India consists of mutually exclusive, endogamous, and hereditary groups, which were traditionally organized around rules related to commensality and ritual purity/pollution, which in turn were linked to the occupations that the specific castes were pursuing. It is important to recognize that this system underwent major transformation through the centuries, and its meaning and *modus operandi* has not been the same at all times, and in all regions (see, for instance, Bayly 1999, Chakravarti 1987, Dirks 2002, and Jaiswal 2000). In its ancient manifestation, the roughly 2,500-year-old varna system, there were four broad groups: Brahmins (often priests, teachers, other knowledge-based activities), Kshatriyas (warriors, often royalty), Vaishyas (traders, retailers, moneylenders), and Shudras (manual jobs). At some point in its evolution, the Shudras split into two groups, giving rise to the group of Ati-Shudras who did the most menial jobs. They were regarded below the line of ritual purity and were regarded as 'untouchables'. These individuals were considered too low to be assigned a varna, and were thus the 'avarna' (sans varna), in contrast to 'savarna'. They were a part of the varna system by being outside its fold or by virtue of being excluded. First references to the practice of untouchability can be seen circa 1020 AD. Thus, even though untouchability arose later than the varna system itself, it is old enough to be considered an integral part of the caste system.

Over time, as the economy grew more complex, and as new castes emerged through fission, fusion, intermarriages, migration, and the emergence of new occupations, the varna system got transformed into the jati system, which is essentially a system of regional caste groupings. While the jati system shares many similarities with the varna system, jatis are not a clear sub-set of varnas. Even the exact number of jatis is not known with certainty—the count is close to 7,000 communities, with a wide variation in sizes, some with more than a million members and others with less than 1,000 members (Singh 1993). The varna–jati link is fluid, except at the very top and bottom. It is also important to note that the link between jati and occupation is less straightforward than that between varna and occupation.

Thus, the jati system should be understood as a system of graded inequality, and not a simple dichotomous hierarchy between 'upper castes' and 'lower castes'. Also, it is important to note that the caste system has not remained static—migration, emulation, isolation, segregation, occupational specialization, conversion, and incorporation of tribal groups—all these factors have resulted in addition, fission, and fusion of castes and changes in their relative standing.

In the contemporary economy, the direct link between caste and traditional occupations is broken to a large extent, as new occupations have proliferated far beyond traditional occupations, and several individuals have moved out of their traditional jati occupations. This has given rise to the widespread belief that the caste system is either dead or irrelevant, substantively speaking, in the sense that it does not affect material outcomes, but merely shapes social or ritual practices. The dissociation between jati and traditional occupations could be happening either due to the fact that traditional occupations themselves are dying, or because there is a total reshuffling of the deck, in that access to different occupations is not linked in any way to individual positions in the caste hierarchy. It turns out that despite the weakening, and in some cases, disappearance of the link between jati and occupation, the overlap between caste and status persists. 'Polluting' jobs are still done by the castes to which they were traditionally assigned, and on the other end of the scale, there is still widespread opposition, for example, to ex-untouchables even entering temples, not to mention virulent opposition to their becoming priests, a job traditionally associated with Brahmins. This is despite the fact that untouchability has been illegal since the foundation of the Indian republic.

Thus, the identification of the ex-untouchable jatis in terms of their placement in the varna scale is relatively more straightforward, as compared to the other jatis, where it is more difficult and controversial to assign them a varna status. In addition to clearly worse economic outcomes discussed later in this chapter, there is plenty of evidence to suggest that ex-untouchable jatis (Ati-Shudras) are subjected to a variety of deprivations, discrimination, oppression, violence, exclusion, and a stigmatized ethnic identity. Having said this, we should note that under the jajmani system—the traditional system of reciprocal obligations under the caste system—there are various rules governing a whole range of social and economic interactions between jatis. Thus, a variety of interactions might be prohibited (or conversely, certain interactions allowed) between a set of jatis. This suggests that untouchability itself is not a dichotomous concept. But there are jatis below the line of ritual purity that, traditionally, would be considered completely untouchable in that all contact with them would be shunned.

## To Count or Not to Count?

Ideally, one would like to see a rigorous and detailed empirical assessment of caste disparities which would help us uncover the truth about what has changed, to what extent, in what direction, and over what period. Here we run into feasibility and data problems. Does one undertake a pair-wise comparison of jatis? This would be mind-boggling and have very low interpretive power, assuming that it is possible at all. The basic hurdle here would be that there is no definitive count of how many castes exist. The 1931 census, which is the most comprehensive jati-based census, contrary to popular belief, actually does not count all castes. The then census commissioner, J.H. Hutton, was an anthropologist who believed that tribals, as also the 'exterior castes' (now the SCs), 'formed a distinct element in the Indian population which was not amenable to normal constitutional processes but which required a strategy of intervention by the government to protect their rights and promote their welfare' (Singh: Foreword to the 1931 Census). This census gave, for the first time, a comprehensive account of the number and distribution of 'primitive tribes', as well as of all exterior castes. Exterior was the new nomenclature for the term 'depressed classes', which was considered derogatory but was used in previous censuses (and continued to be used in official documents later). The 1931 census

15

counted 277 exterior castes, with a population share of 10.1 per cent; the 1981 census counted 504 SC communities with a population share of roughly 16 per cent (Singh 1993). The scope of the 1931 census with regard to other (non-exterior) castes was rather limited. The state census officials were told not to tabulate figures for castes for which the 'Local Government did not regard such tabulation as important', as well as those which fell below a minimal demographic standard for enumeration of castes (Census of India 1931: 432). This resulted in the enumeration of only a dozen or so selected castes. It also used the 1891 census method of grouping castes by their traditional occupations. Despite its limitations, it remains to date the most comprehensive enumeration of castes—1941 was a war-time census and from 1951 onwards, in keeping with the ideal of a 'casteless' India, the national census counted only SCs and STs, the target groups for the AA programme.

The currently ongoing socio-economic census has been highly controversial both at the conceptual level (is it needed at all) and in its operationalization (how data are being collected and therefore what they will yield). The arguments in favour of not counting caste are made in benign or neutral terms, in that it is assumed that counting caste would work towards strengthening vested interests and that it is, therefore, a political exercise (in a pejorative sense), whereas not counting caste is objectively speaking the right course to adopt since it is apolitical. One popular strand of the argument is that counting caste will enhance caste consciousness. The curious fact is that the same argument is never invoked for data on other social categories such as religion and language, both of which have been extremely divisive, and the cause of bloody and heinous conflict, but which continue to get counted. Deshpande and John (2010) argue that far from being a neutral argument, there is a politics to *not* counting caste. Given that the status quo is not neutral, the demand for not counting caste 'has defeated the desire to transcend caste'. They argue that 'half-hearted caste-blindness encouraged and perpetuated the deepening of caste inequalities under a supposedly casteless constitution' (Ibid.: 42).

At the time of writing, the socio-economic census is being carried out and there is no macro-level

17

national data by jati, based on which we can compare the relative position of different jatis. Available national data are defined by the needs of the AA programme which divides the population into initially three, and now four, broad groups: (i) SCs (ex-untouchable jatis), on average about 18 per cent of the Indian population; (ii) STs, on average about 8 per cent of the Indian population; (iii) OBCs (a heterogeneous collection of Hindu low castes, some non-Hindu communities, and some tribes which are not included in STs), not yet counted by the census, but, according to the NSS 66th round (2009–10), constitute 43 per cent of the rural and 39 per cent of the urban population; and (iv) 'Others' (the residual; everyone else). Given that data do not allow us to isolate the upper castes, it needs to be emphasized at the outset that calculations based on this categorization will underestimate the disparity between the two ends of the jati spectrum. While the term 'Scheduled Castes' is a product of this official terminology, several members of the ex-untouchable jatis prefer to self-identify themselves as 'Dalit'—the originally Sanskrit but now Marathi term, meaning 'oppressed' or 'broken', which is used as a term of pride.

# The Case for Caste-based AA in India

The idea of preferential treatment for caste and tribal groups perceived to be the lowest in social and economic hierarchy predates Indian independence. The evolution of preferential policies in the colonial period is discussed in Chapter 2. The Constitution of independent India declared untouchability illegal and espoused the ideal of a casteless society. However, in order to do that it was necessary to identify the groups which bore the brunt of caste inequality both socially and economically. The approach here was a continuation of the preferential treatment policy of the pre-independence days towards groups belonging to the erstwhile depressed classes, the untouchable castes, and marginalized tribes. AA towards these groups was enshrined in the Indian Constitution, the history and details of which are discussed in the next chapter. In this section we discuss the contemporary rationale for AA towards these groups. In other words, given that this policy originated in the early twentieth century, the arguments in favour of AA are not restated as they originated, but are being reiterated with contemporary evidence. As stated at the outset, each of the following points is strongly contested, and Chapter 4 explores the debates in detail.

## *Material Realities are Systematically Related to Caste*

### INTER–CASTE DISPARITIES

Before we examine evidence on disparities in standard of living, we need to understand why the existence of material disparities could possibly constitute an argument in favour of AA, given that quotas are applicable only in elite positions and are not specifically designed to reduce gaps in the standard of living. There is a vicious cycle here: material deprivation makes it harder for individuals from disadvantaged groups to access elite positions, and the lower representation of these groups in high-earning positions keeps their average standard of living down. This vicious cycle needs to be broken at both ends: effective AA can break it at the upper end by making it easier for some individuals to access elite jobs, whereas anti-poverty or livelihood support and/ or health and nutrition-based programmes can break it at the lower end by raising the standard of living of the poor among the disadvantaged communities.

Data from a variety of sources on material standards of living, poverty rates, health status, educational attainment, and occupational outcomes indicate that the disparities between SCs–STs and non-OBC Others (a loose proxy for upper castes) are persistent and systematic, regional variation notwithstanding (Thorat and Newman 2010). Given that income data for India are not very reliable, the monthly per capita consumption expenditure (MPCE) is used as a proxy. Without going into the debate over fixing the poverty line, we can look at the proportion of the different groups in the bottom 40 per cent of the MPCE distribution (a rough approximation of the poor). From the 2009–10 NSS data, we see that these shares are 54.9, 49.9, and 39.8 for STs, SCs, and OBCs, respectively, and 21.2 per cent for 'Others'. Thus, the proportion of SCs–STs in the bottom 40 per cent is roughly 2.5 times that of 'Others'. This is despite the caveat mentioned earlier: that the 'Others' category would have castes very close to SCs–STs in economic position, thus the gap between the top end of the 'Others' and SCs–STs would be far greater. Few would argue with evidence which shows that the proportions of SCs–STs are higher in the bottom 40 per cent of consumption distribution and lower in the top 10 per cent. However, it could be argued that large proportions of Dalits are in the informal sector, where wages are not regulated, earnings are low and erratic, and the possibility of discrimination is greater, but those who make it to regular salaried and wage employment would not face systematic gaps in wages, that is, in the 'modern' jobs for which the anti-Mandal agitationists believed only merit mattered and caste did not matter, except when it was recognized for the purpose of AA.

Looking at average daily wages of social groups, Abraham's (2012) calculations reveal that the ratio of SC wages to 'Others' wages was 0.71 in 1983, which then fell to 0.61 in 2009–10, so the gap between SCs and 'Others' wages *increased* over the last 25 years or so. There is a gender dimension to this story: this increased gap is due to the sharp decline in the ratio of female wages of the two groups (SC women/'Other' women) which fell from 0.86 in 1983 to 0.54 in 2009–10. This is confirmed by the rate of growth of daily wages—this is lower for SCs than for the 'Others', indicating that average wages are diverging rather than converging. The bulk of these jobs are untouched by AA, and yet there is a clear and systematic difference in the distribution of wages *by caste*. This is linked to labour market discrimination, which is discussed subsequently.

While wages or MPCE are a measure of current earnings or income, land is a measure of wealth. In the distribution of landownership, one finds much greater inequality than in the distribution of wages or consumption expenditure. From the 2004–5 NSS data we see that in the aggregate, 'Others', who were 26 per cent of the population owned 36 per cent of the land, as compared to SCs who were 22 per cent but owned 9 per cent of the land. Given the historical restrictions on the ownership of land by Dalits, this figure of 9 per cent appears to be a result of the limited land reforms after independence, some beneficiaries of which have been Dalits. This aggregate figure hides some extreme disparity in some states: in Haryana, SCs who were 29 per cent of the population owned 3 per cent of the land, while 'Others' who were 40 per cent of the population owned 72 per cent of the land.

These figures are indicative but by no means exceptional; more detailed data, for instance, in Deshpande (2011) and Thorat and Newman (2010), confirm the simple fact that gaps between Dalits and upper castes are unambiguous and persistent. Given the rather narrow ambit of AA, these could not possibly be *caused* by AA: these would need to be remedied by targeted interventions, AA being one such intervention.

## *There is Continuing Discrimination against Dalits and Adivasis*

### SOCIAL DISCRIMINATION AGAINST DALITS

Dalits continue to suffer from a 'stigmatized ethnic identity' due to their untouchable past and remain mired in corresponding social backwardness. There is sufficient evidence that amply demonstrates the various aspects of stigmatization, exclusion, rejection, and violence that Dalits continue to face in contemporary India (see, for example, HRW 1999). In rural India, despite the breakdown of the traditional subsistence economy, caste continues to make its strong presence felt in many different dimensions. Shah et al. (2006) document untouchability in rural India based on the results of an extensive survey carried out over 2001–2 in 565 villages across 11 states. They find that untouchability is not only present all over rural India, but it has 'survived by adapting to new socio-economic realities and taking on new and insidious forms' (p. 15). Navsarjan's (2010) is the latest comprehensive study of untouchability in 1,589 villages in Gujarat. It documents 98 types of untouchability practices directed towards Dalits by non-Dalits. These include well-known forms such as preventing Dalits from entering temples, and also a mind-boggling variety of other practices such as Dalits not being allowed to enter a kitchen, even when they are employed as domestic help, or not being allowed to buy or rent houses in non-Dalit residential areas, or public goods such as street lights or municipal taps not being allocated to parts of the village where the Dalits live, or Dalits being required to puff their pipes or cigarettes away from the direction of non-Dalits so that the latter do not get 'defiled' by the smoke. Further, non-Dalit midwives will not offer their services for assisting pregnant Dalit women and when the sarpanch (elected head of the village council), who is supposed to be the chair of the village council, is a Dalit, he will sit on the floor while upper castes sit on benches or chairs. Sharma (2012), in a comprehensive empirical analysis of violence against Dalits over the period 2001–9, finds that violence (murder, arson, destruction of property, rape, assault, bodily harm, and so forth) against Dalits increases when MPCE gaps between Dalits and upper castes decrease. This could be due to upper castes feeling threatened, or a reaction to a perceived unsettling of a natural social hierarchy where Dalits are expected to remain at the bottom of the socio-economic ladder.

There is another aspect of social discrimination which results in gruesome violence against Dalits. This particular aspect arises from the fact that gender plays a critical role in maintaining caste purity: 'the subordination of women was crucial to the development of caste hierarchy, women being subject to increasing constraints the higher the caste in the hierarchy' (Liddle and Joshi 1986: 50). While inter-caste marriages are not very common, the worst social sanctions are reserved for *pratiloma* marriages (lower-caste men marrying upper-caste women). Such marriages, as well as others which do not follow the rigid rules of permissible marriages (for example, same *gotra* marriages) result in a phenomenon called 'honour killings', which is murder in the name of saving family honour (http://www.bbc.co.uk/news/10364986; http://www.honourkilling.in/, accesses on 8 July 2012). Families of the couples, especially of the woman, are actively involved in the killing and this is supported by traditional community/caste courts (for instance, the dreaded *khap* panchayats), which have no legal validity. This is only a small part of the violence and atrocities which Dalits have to face on an everyday basis. Urban India might have fewer overt instances of untouchability, but for a practice which has been outlawed for over six decades, it is remarkably resilient and continues to exist in various forms.

## DISCRIMINATION AGAINST ADIVASIS

The designation of tribals or Adivasis as 'primitive' is a hangover from colonial practices; while the original intention was to demarcate aboriginal groups, the term is used in a sense antithetical to the idea of modernity and is stigmatizing. In independent India, of the 500 groups which are designated as STs, 75 are designated as 'Primitive Tribal Groups' (PTGs) based on their racial characteristics, spatial location, and habitat. The issue of defining appropriate Adivasi rights is complicated

27

and it is important to recognize the nuances in order to comprehend the multiple ways in which Adivasi rights are violated. As Kannabiran (2012) discusses, for nomadic, semi-nomadic, pastoralist tribes and tribes engaged in shifting cultivation, preservation of their distinct lifestyles would mean guaranteeing them freedom to be on the move. Other tribes notified under Schedule V and Schedule VI areas need the guarantee that they will not be evicted from these areas and will be able to pursue traditional livelihoods if they want to.

The stigmatization of tribes began in the early decades of the twentieth century through a process of which the 'primitive' designation was only one aspect. The Criminal Tribes Act of 1911 enabled local governments to declare any tribe or a class of people a 'criminal tribe' and the government could authorize close surveillance and preventive arrests of people from that community. Several nomadic tribes got designated as such, as well as those tribes whose traditional occupations got disrupted with the spread of capitalism (for example, Koravas, an itinerant trading community which traded in grain, salt, cattle, bamboo, and so on, between interior districts and coastal areas in the mid-nineteenth century, became redundant with the spread of the railways and roads). The criminal designation was deeply stigmatizing and even though these tribes have been de-notified, the stigma remains.

The major problem that Adivasis face today is dispossession, with the settlement of non-tribals on tribal land and of forced displacement due to large-scale development projects. The issue is not simply of individual displacement. Even when rehabilitation, inadequate as it is, is undertaken, it does not take into account the loss of community and common and shared spaces, which are integral to their lives. Several Adivasi-dominated areas are extremely rich in forests and natural resources, and hence attractive for large corporations. The battle over control of these resources, with the state often seen to be supporting corporate interests, is another aspect of the process of disentitlement which deepens the sense of tribal alienation. It is not a coincidence that tribal-dominated areas in large parts of the country have been in the throes of an extended Maoist insurgency. The issues involved are complex and difficult to summarize in a few sentences, but existing research (summarized in Deshpande 2012) shows that sustained poverty and underdevelopment and a deep sense of tribal alienation provide a fertile ground for insurgency against the state. Tribals in the north-eastern states (especially those in Assam, Meghalaya, Tripura, and Mizoram) are under Schedule VI of the Indian Constitution which guarantees them autonomy and considerable powers with respect to framing land use policies. When the rights listed in the Constitution are violated or not implemented with seriousness, it leads to suspicion and further alienation and results in escalation of conflict.

### LABOUR MARKET DISCRIMINATION

There is sufficient evidence to indicate that caste disparities in economic outcomes, for instance, in occupational attainment are neither mainly a hangover from the past, nor are they mainly a result of educational or skill gaps. Thus, members of SC–ST communities will face worse employment outcomes *even if they were similarly qualified as the 'Others'*, given discrimination in labour (job) markets (see Madheswaran and Attewell 2007; Deshpande 2011).

Average wages for SCs and Others differ across all occupation categories. The question is whether this difference in average wages simply reflects the differences in education and skill levels between the two groups or whether the wage gap persists even after human capital or endowment differences have been accounted for. Also, what needs to be determined is whether labour markets display *job discrimination* (wages differ because the two groups end up in different parts of the job spectrum) or *wage discrimination* (wages differ because members of groups get paid differently in the same job), or both, in which case, which of the two might be more important. Thus, there are studies which have decomposed the wage gap into two components: 'explained' (by wage earning characteristics which include human capital and skill characteristics) and 'unexplained' or 'discriminatory'—that part of the wage gap which remains even after all possible wage earning characteristics are accounted for.

It is important to note that the so-called 'explained' or non-discriminatory part already contains a discriminatory component. The fact that the two groups enter the labour market with substantial differences in education levels indicates 'pre-market discrimination', which means that there are discriminatory factors at work in the formative years which prevent Dalits from acquiring the same quantity and quality of education as the upper castes. There is plenty of evidence which documents the substantial gaps between SCs and 'Others' in access to education, quality of education, attitude of teachers, and access to resources that could enhance learning and also of active discrimination inside schools (Nambissan 2010). Hanna and Linden (2009) conducted an experiment to measure discrimination in educational contexts. They ran an exam competition in which children competed for a financial prize. They then changed the cover sheet of the exam randomly and assigned to each sheet 'child characteristics' (age, gender, and caste), such that there was no systematic relationship between actual performance and characteristics of the child. With these new cover sheets, they gave the exam scripts to school teachers to grade. They found that teachers tended to give scripts marked low-caste and female lower scores compared to those marked high caste and male.

The reason this is called 'pre-market' discrimination is that all of this has already occurred by the time individuals seek jobs in the labour market. Hypothetically, suppose there is no active labour market discrimination. In that case, all job seekers will get jobs according to their human capital characteristics, subject to demand of course, in which case too, Dalits will fare worse than the upper castes. However, these disparities will be due to 'pre-market' discrimination. What the decomposition studies find is that labour markets actively discriminate, which means even when the differences in characteristics such as education, skill, occupation, and sector are accounted for, there is a part of the wage gap which cannot be accounted for.

The evidence on persistence of caste-based discrimination in rural labour markets is perhaps not as surprising as evidence from urban job markets, especially in modern, formal sector employment. This is because individuals are more easily identified by their caste status in rural areas and presumably are more inclined to pursue caste-based occupations, given the correspondingly lower spread of the modern, formal economy. Caste is supposed to be anonymous in urban settings; identification of caste is difficult, since it is not phenotypically ascriptive. Additionally, urban markets are supposed to respond to 'merit', so even if hypothetically caste could be identified, it is not supposed to matter.

However, recent evidence on urban labour market discrimination (Madheswaran and Attewell 2007), based on NSS data from 1983 to 2000, suggests, first, that human capital, or skill differences between SCs and non-SCs have been narrowing since the 1980s. Thus, *ceteris paribus*, if urban markets were free of discrimination, wage gaps should be narrower. However, over the same period, raw wage differentials increased overall. Also, the study indicates that SCs–STs have lower rate of return to education at all levels, which means that the labour market values the same educational characteristics differently for the two groups. It is job discrimination which turns out to be very important: discrimination operates through occupational segregation. Their results indicate that of the gross wage difference, 24.9 per cent is explained by endowment differences (due to educational and skill level differences, among other things); 18.6 per cent by occupational differences (the fact that SCs and 'Others' are concentrated in different parts of the occupational spectrum due to their differential human capital levels); 20.9 per cent by wage discrimination (SCs and 'Others' earn different wages for the same job after taking into account their differential characteristics); and 35.4 per cent by job discrimination (SCs and 'Others' are concentrated in different parts of the occupational distribution, for reasons not explained by their human capital characteristics).

Following the seminal study by Bertrand and Mullainathan (2003), in the first major correspondence study in India, Thorat and Attewell (2007), sent out *exactly identical* resumes to private companies, both domestic and multinational corporations (MNCs), in response to newspaper adverstisements in New Delhi during 2005–6. The only difference in the resumes were the easily identifiable names of applicants and three categories were used: Hindu upper caste, Hindu Dalit, and Muslims. So for each job advertisement, several sets (of three identically matched resumes) were sent and the idea was to see how many candidates were called for an interview. This would only demonstrate the intention to hire on the part of employers, not reveal what the actual hiring would have been. But given that the resumes were exactly the same (including extra-curricular actvities) and that the companies had not seen these candidates, on paper, there was nothing to distinguish one applicant from another, except their names. If qualifications were the only thing that mattered, then either all the applicants from a given set of resumes would be called for an interview, or none would be. However, the study revealed significant differences in call-backs between Hindu upper castes and the other two categories. Dalit applicants' chances of a call-back were 0.67 that of Hindu upper castes, whereas Muslims fared even worse with their chances of call-back being 0.33 that of the Hindu upper castes. Siddique (2009) conducted a correspondence study in Chennai during 2006 for jobs posted online which has similar findings. This study sent out two resumes for each job, one with typically high-caste names and the second with low-caste names. She finds that high-caste applicants had a 20 per cent higher chance of being called back. Testing for the interaction between caste and gender, she finds that the effect of being low caste for female applicants reduces the call-back probability by 37 per cent.

Both international evidence as well as economic theory suggest that discrimination is compatible with a market economy. There are studies of hiring practices which emphasize the role of networks and that of informal and personalized recruitment, where 'who you know' is often more important than 'what you know' (Deshpande and Newman 2007; Royster 2003). In a college-to-work study, which tried to uncover the exact pathways through which discrimination manifests itself, Deshpande and Newman (2007) tracked a group of students from the three premier Indian universities in Delhi for two years trying to understand what jobs they got, how they got them, and what their interview experiences were. It turned out that employers were extremely conscious of the social identity of the applicant, all the while professing deep allegiance only to the 'merit' of the candidate.

There is widespread prevalence of personalized recruitment. Employers find this convenient and 'efficient'; for them, it minimizes recruitment costs, ensures commitment and loyalty, and minimizes transaction costs of disciplining workers and handling disputes and grievances. Jodhka and Newman (2007), in an employer attitude survey, find that employers, including MNCs, universally use the language of merit. However, managers are blind to the unequal playing field which produces 'merit'. Commitment to merit is voiced alongside convictions that merit is distributed by caste and region. Thus, qualities of individuals are replaced by stereotypes that, at best, will make it harder for a highly qualified job applicant to gain recognition for his/her skills and accomplishments.

In view of the unambiguous evidence on discrimination, AA becomes essential to guarantee representation to Dalits in preferred positions. It should be noted, however, that AA in India, due to the specific forms it takes, is not a complete remedy for discrimination, if not for any other reason than the fact that AA is applicable only to the public sector, whereas the evidence of discrimination is overwhelmingly from the private sector, which is becoming increasingly important in the Indian economy.

## *Economic Inequality between Castes Leads to Inequality of Opportunity*

The preceding discussion makes it clear that in contemporary India, caste defines and shapes life chances in multiple ways. The claim of castelessness or the belief that caste does not matter can only be made by those whose lives are not impaired by their caste status and typically, these are the upper-caste, urban elite. Dalits and upper castes not only have unequal outcomes, but Dalits cannot access or are denied the same opportunities as the upper castes. Given that opportunities are so unequal, outcomes will necessarily be unequal, even if there were no active discrimination in labour, credit, land, or consumer markets. Thus, AA is seen necessary to equalize opportunities in certain positions.

It should be noted that equality of opportunity as a philosophical concept is not opposed to hierarchy per se, but to caste hierarchy. In other words, there is recognition of the fact that final outcomes might be unequal due to differential abilities, but if individual chances are affected not by abilities but by birth into particular castes, then the resulting inequality is seen as unfair. Thus, equality of opportunity allows for a situation where everyone has an equal chance to compete for all positions and the resultant inequality is not an outcome of birth, but reflects the results of a fair competition.

It should be clear that economic inequality is a threat to equality of opportunity. Those who are born poor cannot compete as effectively as the well-off for desirable positions because their families cannot give them the same level of education, network support, healthcare, the same level of cultural capital, and so forth. Thus, even if there was no discrimination, the poor do not have equal opportunities as the rich.

Translating this argument to caste inequality, one can say that AA in education or entry-level jobs is needed to provide a level playing field to members of SC–ST communities, to compensate them for the heavy load of disadvantage vis-à-vis the upper castes due to clear inter-caste inequality in initial conditions. With this perspective, Indian AA can be seen as a system of compensatory discrimination.

## Compensation for Historical Wrongs

Finally, (arguably) social policy ought to compensate for the historical wrongs of a system that generated systematic disparity between caste groups and actively kept untouchables at the very bottom of the social and economic order. This argument has been used forcefully in certain international contexts. For instance, in Australia, where the children of the Australian aboriginal and Torres Strait Islander populations were forcibly removed from their families by government agencies and church missions approximately between 1869 and 1969, the issue of compensation for this 'stolen generation' is a very potent one. The formal apology by the Prime Minister of Australia, Kevin Rudd, in 2008 to indigenous Australians is the recognition of the harm inflicted on entire generations of aboriginals due to this heinous, racially discriminatory practice. However, the suggestion that the apology should translate into formal compensation for the harm is seriously contested, even as individual cases of compensation are being considered by the courts.

In South Africa, a Truth and Reconciliation Commission (TRC) was set up to help deal with the violence and human rights abuses during Apartheid. One of the issues under TRC's ambit was that of reparations: the Commission could consider any form of reparations which would be sustainable and would help individual victims of human rights abuses as well as communities whose 'dignity was destroyed through a systematic machinery of human rights violations and state neglect'. Reparations could include any form of compensation, ex gratia payment, restitution, rehabilitation, or recognition and the victims were defined as persons who suffered harm in the form of 'physical injury, mental injury, emotional suffering, pecuniary loss and substantial impairment of human rights'. Recently, this demand is being forcefully made in the context of reparations to the descendants of former slaves in the US.

41

However, given the complex and long history of the Indian subcontinent, the use of this argument in the context of caste-based oppression and untouchability has to proceed with extreme caution, as several right-wing outfits invoke completely unsubstantiated, often manufactured injustices against the so-called indigenous inhabitants and ask for compensation for historical wrongs. For a region marked by large waves of migration over centuries, it is not clear who the original inhabitants of the region are. As the Babri Masjid mosque dispute illustrates, the definition of historical 'wrongs' is a site marked by bitter contestation and, therefore, the question of compensation is a fraught one. Coming to gross violations against particular groups resulting from centuries of untouchability, the argument of compensation for historical wrongs could be, and has been, used as one of the elements in the case for AA. However, the case itself does not rest on this argument and can be made just as forcefully even without this particular element. In other words, the case for AA as a compensation for contemporary exclusion is just as strong, even if one did not view it as necessary to remedy historical exclusion.

A Brief History of the Evolution of
Preferential Treatment during the
Colonial Period

## 2

# The Past and Present of the Affirmative Action Programme in India

'On the 26th January 1950, we are going to enter into a life of contradictions. In politics we will have equality and in social and economic life we will have inequality. In politics we will be recognising the principle of one man one vote and one vote one value. In our social and economic life, we shall by reason of our social and economic structure, continue to deny the principle of one man one value. How long shall we continue to live this life of contradictions?'

—B.R. Ambedkar,
Speech to the Constituent Assembly,
25 November 1949

# A Brief History of the Evolution of Preferential Treatment during the Colonial Period

In the nineteenth century, after the British consolidated their hold on substantial parts of the subcontinent, their policy was one of 'non-interference', which meant recognition of the established social order, but no conscious attempt to change it. Galanter (1984) discusses, with specific examples, how the policy of non-interference was not neutral in consequence, in that both the conscious actions and aloofness of the British had an impact on Indian society. The establishment of a nationwide legal system was one such example, as the principle of equality before the law which was implicit in this legal system generated a dynamic of its own, and the various Hindu reform movements, which were already underway, as well as caste organizations used the concept of formal equality to gradually articulate demands which often amounted to questioning caste hierarchy and inequality. Prakash (1997: 39) argues that, for instance, in many parts of the Madras Presidency, one of the consequences of the explicit Brahmin dominance at the regional level was the 'attempt by

44

the educated and professional sections of other castes to mobilise their caste associations'. This formed the backdrop to the formation of the Justice Party and the demand for reservations for non-Brahmins.

However, the progress of anti-caste and anti-untouchability movements was uneven. For instance, in 1856, a Mahar boy who was refused admission to a government school appealed to the Bombay Education Department, but his appeal was rejected on the grounds that it would not be useful to alienate the vast majority of students on account of one boy. In 1858, the Government of Bombay Presidency announced that it had the right to refuse support to any school which withheld benefits of education to any person on account of caste and race (Galanter 1984: 20–1; Vijayan 2006: 46). However, these legal safeguards were not always effective in the face of stiff opposition from high-caste families.

These kinds of legal changes provided a fillip to a wide variety of social reform movements, from anti-caste to missionary reformers. Among the prominent anti-caste movements in the nineteenth century was one led by Jotiba Phule, who along with his wife Savitribai, focused on education for untouchables, especially untouchable girls, supported widow remarriage, and opposed child marriage. Another important movement started in the early twentieth century under the aegis of the non-Brahmin Justice Party (for a detailed discussion of these movements, see Deshpande 2011). All these developments propelled untouchability as one of the major concerns on the national stage and the question of some form of preferential treatment towards the 'depressed classes', as they were known then, was seen as critical where most notably, Ambedkar carried forward the concerns of his predecessor anti-caste social reformers to ensure political safeguards for the depressed classes.

The preferential policies of the British state towards untouchables were followed by several progressive rulers of princely states, for example, in Baroda, Kolhapur, and Travancore, who introduced reservations in administrative positions for backward classes in the first quarter of the twentieth century. In addition to reservations, both types of territories, British-ruled as well as princely states, introduced legislation which targeted untouchability as a major social disability arising out of the caste system, for example, the Maharaja of Travancore's Temple Entry Proclamation of 1936, the Madras Removal of Civil Disabilities Act of 1938, the Bombay Harijan Temple Entry Act of 1943, the United Provinces Removal of Social Disabilities Act of 1947, and so forth.

There were two broad approaches to untouchability that dominated public discourse in the first half of the twentieth century: first, the evangelical one, which was espoused by Mahatma Gandhi, emphasized 'moral regeneration and philanthropic uplift' (Galanter 1984: 28). Gandhi was not opposed to the caste system (the varnashrama dharma) per se, but to its extreme and ugly side: untouchability. He campaigned for the de-ostracization of the untouchables, and called them 'Harijans'—people close to god. He advocated inter-marriages and championed dignity of all labour as a key to lowering caste taboos and expressed a desire to be reborn as an untouchable. But he celebrated the idealized village community, based on the varna system as a benign division of labour and his campaign against untouchability was aimed at restoring Hinduism to its pristine, benign, ideal form, where the untouchables would be restored to their rightful place in the varna order—that of being Shudras. Gandhi's view of the caste system differed very sharply from that of Phule's

47

and Ambedkar's and of the other critics of the caste system, notably Periyar. Ambedkar (1945) wrote a scathing criticism of Gandhi in his book *What Congress and Gandhi Have Done to the Untouchables*. A detailed discussion of their differences is outside the scope of this book but this quote from Gandhi illustrates the sharp contrast.

> In a visit to south India in 1927, seemingly oblivious to the spread of the anti-Brahmin movement, Gandhi publicly declared: 'Varnashrama dharma is not an unmitigated evil but it is one of the foundations on which Hinduism is built [and it] defines man's mission on earth ... Brahmins [are the] finest flowers of Hinduism and humanity', adding that he would 'do nothing to wither it'. (Pandian 2007: 191)

The other, the secular approach of B.R. Ambedkar, which carried forward the sharp critique articulated by Phule, Periyar E.V. Ramasamy Naicker, and others, rejected the caste system outright on the grounds that untouchability was one of the pillars of the caste system. For instance, he believed that Hindus who were practising untouchability were simply observing their ritual duties, not deviating from prescribed behaviour.

He rejected the possibility of any change of heart or reform within Hinduism which would abolish the caste system, and thus stressed the urgency of civic and economic improvement in the condition of untouchables under government auspices. In contrast to Gandhi who idealized the self-sufficient village community, in his introduction to the draft Constitution in the constituent assembly in November 1948, Ambedkar argued that the village was a '... sink of localism, a den of ignorance, narrow mindedness and communalism' (quoted in Rodrigues 2002: 486).

The debate between Gandhi and Ambedkar started in the Indian National Congress, and along with this debate, the rise of non-Brahmin parties in various parts of the British territory, especially in the southern regions, precipitated the provision of some measure of preferential treatment as compensation or support to the untouchables. In several of these instances, partly due to the influence of thinkers and leaders such as Periyar E.V. Ramasamy Naicker or Jotiba Phule, the dichotomy between Brahmins and the larger collective of Shudra–Ati-Shudras was emphasized as the key contradiction of the caste system. This view not only shaped the nature of anti-caste movements, but also influenced the formulation of preferential schemes. For instance, in 1918 the princely state of Mysore defined all groups other than Brahmins as 'backward classes' and reserved places for them in colleges and state services, the first instance of quotas in the Indian sub-continent. This was meant to redress a situation where Brahmins, who were roughly 3 per cent of the population, extensively dominated elite positions—civil-service jobs and related prestigious jobs. For instance, in 1918, 65 per cent of all gazetted posts and 70 per cent of all non-gazetted posts in Mysore state services were occupied by Brahmins (Dushkin 1979: 662). The Government of India Act of 1919 accorded a few nominated seats to non-Brahmins in the political arena. In 1926, provisions similar to the ones in Mysore were enacted in Bombay and Madras Presidencies, which were directly under British rule. The Justice Party in Madras undertook a systematic effort to redistribute public positions to non-Brahmin communities, and the 1926 quotas in Madras for public appointments were established according to the following rule: every 15 appointments were supposed to be allocated as follows: two to Brahmins, two to 'backward' (low caste) Hindus, six to other Hindus, two to depressed (untouchable) castes, two to Anglo-Indians and Christians, and one to a Muslim (Weisskopf 2004: 11).

The use of quotas as an instrument of preferential policies was actively pursued during the colonial period in both British-ruled areas and in the princely states. In the 1930s, the question of preferential policies in the political arena came to the fore when the British initiated a larger process to establish federal and provincial assemblies to which Indians could elect representatives. The question of separate electorates for specific communities was hotly debated both within and among Indian political formations such as the Indian National Congress, Muslim League, and so forth. In the Second Round Table Conference in 1931, Gandhi, representing the Congress Party, rejected the other Congress members as unrepresentative. In particular, he attacked Ambedkar's claim of representing the untouchables: 'I claim myself, in my own person, to represent the vast mass of the untouchables' (Galanter 1984: 31). Ambedkar drafted a set of political safeguards for the depressed classes, which he submitted along with Rao Bahadur R. Srinivasan, to the sub-committee on minorities of the Round Table Conference. These safeguards included equal citizenship, free enjoyment of equal rights, protection against discrimination, adequate representation in the legislatures and services, redress against prejudicial action or neglect of interests, and so forth. This scheme eventually became the basis for the various constitutional and legal provisions against untouchability (Rodrigues 2002). This round table culminated in the formation of separate electorates for Muslims, Christians, Sikhs, and Anglo-Indians. While Gandhi was opposed to the principle of separate electorates altogether, he conceded the idea for these communities, but resolutely rejected the proposal for untouchables and 'vowed to resist it with his life' (Galanter 1984).

Gandhi carried out his vow by starting a fast unto death, which eventually lasted 21 days. The British government wanted the consent of the affected groups before announcing the final award; in particular, it was important that Ambedkar, as the representative of the depressed classes, agree to this award. Finally, under pressure, Ambedkar relinquished the claim of separate electorates, but got a system of reserved seats for untouchables to be elected from joint or common electorates. The final agreement was reached in 1932 in the

Poona or the Yeravada Pact. The Poona Pact provided 148 seats for untouchables, instead of the 78 separately elected members given by the Communal Award. It also provided a system of primary elections for those reserved seats; a panel of four candidates was to be chosen by electors from the depressed classes (Galanter 1984: 32). This was reflected in the Government of India Act of 1935, which established the new federal and provincial assemblies.

As a result of these events, the issue of preferential treatment for untouchables and, more broadly, the principle that the state should actively play a role in fighting the scourge of untouchability came centre stage. The new provincial governments, which took office in 1937, expanded the scope of the role of the state in fighting untouchability. For instance, Madras passed the first legislation imposing criminal penalties for prohibiting untouchables from the use of public facilities. Earlier, a few princely states had already formally opened temple entry to untouchables. In 1938, for the first time, temple entry acts were passed in Bombay and Madras, as discussed earlier in the chapter.

# AA in Independent India

India became independent in 1947, with a partition of the country which resulted in the formation of Pakistan, carving out Muslim majority areas from Punjab and Bengal into a new country. The new Indian nation embraced the ideal of a secular, casteless society and ensured that the new Constitution reflected this orientation. Ambedkar became the country's first law minister as well as the chairman of the drafting committee of the Constitution.

The basic issue was to balance the principle of 'equality in law' with that of 'equality in fact'. While the former would prohibit any special schemes based on caste, religion, or any other communal marker, the latter would recognize that certain groups or communities were severely disadvantaged or discriminated against and would thus enact provisions which would remove or reduce disparities, such that society moved towards 'equality in fact'. In other words, while Indian law guarantees equal treatment to all citizens, irrespective of social group, the question is whether, in fact, individuals are treated equally under the prevailing social norms and institutions. It was clear to Ambedkar that merely the formal espousal of the principle of 'equality in law' would not actually overcome generations of cumulative disadvantages. Thus, to promote the advancement of untouchables and other 'socially and economically backward classes', in his role as the principle architect of the Constitution, he ensured that constitutional provisions safeguarded the rights of untouchables and protected their interests through preferential policies.

There is tension between the two principles of 'equality in law' and 'equality in fact', and the provisions of the Indian Constitution reflect this tension. To ensure the former, the Constitution ensures fundamental rights such as the guarantee to all citizens of equality before law (Article 14); the prohibition of discrimination on grounds of religion, race, sex, caste or place of birth (Article 15); and the assurance of equality of opportunity in matters of public employment (Article 16). To ensure the provision of 'equality in fact', the Constitution needed to depart from the principle of formal equality and institute the principle of *compensatory discrimination* for groups who were otherwise subjected to social and economic discrimination. Thus we have Article 46, a 'Directive Principle of State

Policy', which states: 'The State shall promote with special care the educational and economic interests of the weaker sections of the people, and, in particular, or the Scheduled Castes and the Scheduled Tribes, and shall protect them from social injustice and all forms of exploitation.'

The implementation of this article has mainly been in the form of preferences in public sector jobs, educational institutions, in the electoral sphere, as well as in special provisions in various development expenditures. The specific clauses of the Constitution which outline these special policies are now listed.

## Reservations in Employment

The Constitution bans discrimination in government employment through Article 16(4) and allows the state to make: '…any provision for the reservation of appointments or posts in favour of any backward class of citizens which, in the opinion of the State, is not adequately represented in the services under the State'.

Clause 4A of the same Article enables the state to provide to reservation to Scheduled Castes (SCs) and Scheduled Tribes (STs) in matters of promotion.

Moreover, Article 335 asserts that the 'claims of the SCs and STs shall be taken into consideration, consistent with the maintenance of efficiency of administration, in the making of appointments to services and posts in connection with the affairs of the Union or of the State'.

The concrete implementation of these articles has been through reservation of seats, or quotas, in government employment for SCs and STs. Between 1947 and 1970, of the posts recruited directly on an all-India basis by open competitive examination, 12.5 per cent were reserved for SCs and 5 per cent for STs. These were raised to 15 and 7.5 per cent in 1970 (a total of 22.5 per cent), which is the level of current reservation for these groups.

All states, except Odisha, Madhya Pradesh, and Jammu and Kashmir had reservations in effect since 1951. In several states, these reservations were part of wider reservations for Other Backward Classes (the present day SC–ST–OBC together were the erstwhile depressed classes), but after 1951, states were asked to separate the two categories (SCs–STs and OBCs). Even though the reservation at the central level—which was 17.5 per cent to begin with and was later raised to

22.5 per cent—reflected the share of the combined SC–ST population at the national level, several states have had varying (typically higher) levels of quotas than what was mandated by the Centre. At the state level, the variation in the proportion of reserved seats is not necessarily in proportion to population shares. For instance, Tamil Nadu has close to 70 per cent quotas, with 18 per cent for SCs and 1 per cent for STs; Rajasthan has 68 per cent, including 14 per cent for 'forward' castes.

## *Reservations in Education*

The Constitution also prohibits discrimination on grounds of religion, race, caste, sex, or place of birth (Article 15), and discrimination in government-aided educational institutions (Article 29[2]). There were two Supreme Court judgments rejecting compensatory discrimination in educational institutions, where the court ruled that while the government was empowered to ensure education for backward classes, it could not do so on grounds of caste. In the 1951 *State of Madras v. Champakam Dorairajan* case, a Brahmin student who did not get admission into a medical college because of caste quotas, but would have been admitted otherwise, sued on the grounds that the quota policy violated Article 29[2] of the Constitution which stipulates that no student shall be denied admission to any educational institution on grounds of caste. The court ruled in favour of the student. As a response to this ruling, within two months of the decision, the Parliament passed the first Constitutional Amendment by amending Article 15 to include a new section to this Article.

Thus, the new section 4 of Article 15 explicitly stated that: 'Nothing in Article 15 or Article 29(2)...shall prevent the State from making any special provision for the advancement of any socially and educationally backward classes of citizens or for the Scheduled Castes and the Scheduled Tribes.'

Under Article 15(4), reservations have been provided in higher-educational institutions for SCs–STs, mirroring quotas in employment. Other than quotas, there is a whole range of special provisions, designed to enable members of target groups to take advantage of the quotas. These include age concessions (that is, relaxation of the minimum age for entry into the service), fee concessions (either in the form of waiver or reduction), and reduction in the minimum qualifying marks for admission. The idea behind these provisions is to reduce or remove some of the barriers which might hinder the ability of target groups to take advantage of the quotas and to make a greater proportion of the target groups eligible for quotas. In addition to the quotas in employment and education, Article 275 requires the central government to provide separate allocations in national development plans for the improvement of SC and ST communities.

### Identification of SCs

The category of 'exterior castes' (now SCs) originated to serve the needs of preferential policies started by the British. At the conceptual level, it was supposed to capture the 'untouchables', groups who on account of their low ritual status were subject to a range of disabilities. However, the exact identification of these groups has gone through several iterations, starting from the beginning of the twentieth century and resulting in a variety of estimates (reported in Galanter 1984). The most elaborate effort to identify untouchables was made by J.H. Hutton, the 1931 Census Commissioner.

He proposed a series of tests to identify untouchable communities, which were designed around the incidence of disabilities:

1.   Whether the caste or class in question can be served by Brahmins or not.
2.   Whether the caste or class in question can be served by barbers, water carriers, tailors, and so on, who serve caste Hindus.
3.   Whether the caste in question pollutes a high-caste Hindu by contact or proximity.
4.   Whether the caste or class in question is one from whose hands a caste Hindu can take water.
5.   Whether the caste or class in question is debarred from using public conveniences such as roads, ferries, wells, or schools.
6.   Whether the caste or class in question is debarred from the use of Hindu temples.
7.   Whether in ordinary social intercourse a well-educated member of the caste or class in question will be treated as an equal by high-caste men of the same educational qualifications.
8.   Whether the caste or class in question is merely depressed on account of its own ignorance,

illiteracy, or poverty and but for that would be subject to no social disability.

9. Whether it is depressed on account of the occupation followed, and whether but for that occupation it would be subject to no social disability.

As can be appreciated, several of these criteria are not easy to observe (for example, 7) or framed in a way such that the answer might not reveal the extent of disability (for example, 5—roads or schools are typically free for anyone to *use*, but for untouchables, the usage might be restricted in some form, and there might be some wells from which the untouchables are barred, but not from certain other wells). A question like 9 is problematic too, given that, often times, the specific occupation is what makes the caste group untouchable or gives it a low ritual status.

The lack of any single test to determine untouchability led to huge debates. However, Ambedkar pointed out that the aim was to identify groups which suffer the contempt and aversion of high-caste Hindus and he warned that 'it is a fatal mistake to suppose that differences in tests of untouchability indicate differences in the conditions of untouchables' (quoted in

Galanter 1984: 129). After considerable debate, denial of access to temples and causing pollution by touch or approach were taken as the generally accepted tests of untouchability and groups in this category were listed in a government schedule in 1936. This list reflected a combination of economic and educational criteria to determine untouchability. In the 1941 census, these groups were 19 per cent of the Hindu population and 12.6 per cent of the total population of undivided India.

After independence, the same approach of identifying untouchables was carried forward. A Scheduled Castes Order was promulgated by the President in 1950 which was a restatement of the 1936 list. The major additions were four Sikh castes and the extension of the list to areas which previously had not compiled a list. There were other changes made to the list between 1951 and 1970, and according to the 1971 census, SCs were 14.6 per cent of the population. As Galanter (1984) elaborates, the changes to the list have been in the form of additions or corrections of groups, rather than being any further attempt to reformulate criteria to determine which groups should be in the schedule. It is important to note that other than caste, two other factors determine which groups should be a part of the SC list—territory and religion. SCs are listed by state and other than Sikh untouchables, only Hindu castes are included. There has been a forceful demand for the inclusion of neo-Buddhists (untouchables who converted to Buddhism) and Dalit Christians, which has not been accepted. Before the 1936 order, the recognition existed that Muslims and Christians, within their religions, contained depressed classes that should be considered for inclusion into the SC list. However, in the disputes leading to the formation of the 1936 list, castes/communities from other religions were not included in the SC list and that situation has prevailed since then, despite periodic demands to the contrary.

### Identification of STs

Designation of groups as STs has been much less controversial than the designation of SCs or OBCs (discussed below). Again, conceptually, this category is supposed to include all those with 'tribal characteristics' (social, religious, linguistic, and cultural distinctiveness), who are spatially and culturally isolated from the mainstream. However, the demarcation between 'tribals' and non-tribals is not unambiguous. Indeed, during the 1950s, some groups which were earlier classified as SCs got reclassified as STs.

The formal mechanism of being listed as a Scheduled Tribe is the same as that for Scheduled Castes. The President consults with the governors of states to designate particular communities as SCs or STs. Once the list is promulgated, it can be changed only by an Act of Parliament. In addition to listing tribal groups in the schedule, there are other specific provisions for tribals which are absent in the case of OBCs or SCs. The British started the policy of insulating certain areas (called Excluded Areas or Partially Excluded Areas in the Government of India Act of 1935) to protect aboriginal people from 'exploitative or demoralizing contact with more sophisticated outsiders' (Galanter 1984: 147). This continued after independence in a policy to designate certain areas as Scheduled Areas, under the Fifth and Sixth Schedules of the Constitution, respectively. The designation of Scheduled Areas is also done by the President, who retains the power to alter or de-schedule them.

The idea behind these supplementary provisions for tribals is to enable them to maintain their distinctiveness, rather than encourage their assimilation with the rest of society. Article 339(2) provides for direct central control over administration; Article 275(1) provides for direct central financial responsibility; Fifth Schedule 3 asks for annual reports from the Governors to the President; Fifth Schedule 4 provides extensive executive power over Scheduled Areas in order to protect them from illegal transfer of their land and to insulate them from private moneylenders; finally, Fifth Schedule 5 asks for the formation of Tribal Advisory Councils to participate in the formulation of policy. The Sixth Schedule contains wide ranging recommendations, as mentioned in the previous chapter, relating to the ability of the autonomous regions and autonomous districts to frame land-use policies, policies related to reserved forests, related to inheritance and marriage rules, and other important determinants of social and economic life in the areas under the Sixth Schedule.

## OBC Reservations

Earlier in this chapter, we discussed preferential policies for the depressed classes in parts of British India, which included communities which were classified as 'backward', as well as the untouchables, tribals, and some non-Hindu communities. Even though there were preferential policies for 'backward classes', their exact definition had not been clearly articulated and details of the various definitions during the British period are spelt out in Galanter (1984). The Constitution of independent India did not define OBCs in a specific way either. However, after the SCs were listed as a separate category, the term 'backward classes' started being used in two senses: as a group of all communities which needed preferential treatment and as castes low in the socio-economic hierarchy, but not as low as the untouchables (presumably the erstwhile Shudras). As should be clear, the two usages overlap considerably. However, given the ambiguity surrounding the varna–jati linkage, the exact identification of groups and communities which should be counted as OBCs has been fraught with a great deal of controversy.

As the constituent assembly debated the use of the term 'backward', the final agreement was that the backward classes other than the SCs and STs would be designated at the local level. Galanter (1984: 161) suggests that part of the reason for not bringing out a central list of OBCs then could have been the belief that the OBCs were a sufficiently potent political force at the local level 'to look out for their own interests', and unlike the untouchables, 'central control of their designation was not required to ensure the inclusion of the deserving'.

Even before the Constitution came into effect, several states formed the category for the first time (for example, Bihar in 1947 and Uttar Pradesh in 1948) and conferred benefits on them, while those states which already had benefits for backward castes, expanded their existing range. Thus, we see that in 1978, without any central reservations for OBCs, at least 13 states reserved seats for backward classes, other than SCs and STs. These reservations were found throughout southern India, in Maharashtra and Gujarat and in parts of north India, with the heaviest representation in the south (Galanter 1984: 87).

The first Backward Classes Commission (with Kaka Kalelkar as its chairman) was established in 1953, which was directed to first determine the criteria which should be adopted to ascertain whether any section of the population could be considered backward (over and above SCs and STs), then, according to these criteria, prepare a list of such classes. The Commission prepared a list of 2,399 groups, which were roughly 32 per cent of the population. It was generally understood that the classes identified by the Commission would be castes or communities. This meant that backwardness was defined or understood in terms of 'social hierarchy based on caste'. Thus the Commission listed as criteria of backwardness trade and occupation, security of employment, educational attainment, representation in government service, and position in social hierarchy.

Much like the contemporary experience, there was a rush among communities wanting to be classified as backward due to the potential benefits that this status would confer upon them. However, in deciding on the validity of these multiple claims, the Commission was stymied by the lack of data. On the one hand, embracing the ideal of a casteless society had led to the conclusion that caste had to be de-emphasized in various spheres, including in the census; on the other hand, combating backwardness or marginalization based on low-caste origins required a clear identification of the marginalized, whether individuals or groups, and for that more data were needed, not less. This dilemma between the urge to de-emphasize caste, but the need to collect more caste-based data to assess what had changed and to what extent, resonates very strongly in the debate that arose when the proposal to count caste was mooted for the 2011 census (discussed in Chapter 1).

Despite the lack of data, the Commission made wide-ranging recommendations for benefits to be conferred to backward classes, often relying on just the names of the caste to make its case. However, at the last minute the chairman repudiated the report of the Commission by stating that he found the use of caste antithetical to democracy and to the eventual creation of a casteless and classless society. Due to several factors (the rush of communities wanting to be classified as backward, the unreliability of data, the extensive recommendations of the commission), the work of the Commission was widely criticized. The basic point of contention was the use of caste or community as the chief axis to determine backwardness. There was a forceful plea made to use economic criteria alone to determine backwardness, and hence to determine *individuals* who could be considered backward on the basis of objective economic criteria, rather than *groups* such as castes or communities, and/or social criteria. In

1965, when the report was finally tabled in Parliament, the central government firmly opposed the definition of backwardness on the basis of communal criteria (that is, communities or castes), arguing that the use of caste was administratively unworkable and was contrary to the 'first principles of social justice' in its exclusion of other poor. The Centre decided not to impose a uniform criterion on the states, but persuaded them to use economic criteria, rather than community-based ones, to identify the backward.

Various state governments set up Backward Classes Commissions and some followed economic criteria endorsed by the Centre. However, most states placed greater emphasis on the caste criterion. The socialist parties in north India, under the ideological leadership of Ram Manohar Lohia, consistently championed quotas for backward castes to the tune of 60 per cent. His famous slogan '*sansopa ne bandhi gaath, pichhda pave sau mein satth*' (Sansopa [the Samyukta Socialist Party] is determined, the backward should get 60 out of 100) became a major rallying point for mobilizing backward castes. Accordingly, the Janata Party government, which was a coalition dominated by various hues of socialists and Lohiaites, set up a commission under the chairmanship of B.P. Mandal in 1978 to examine the entire issue of backwardness, starting with determining the criteria that should be used for identifying the backward.

The Mandal Commission used 11 indicators of social and economic criteria, which were grouped under three heads: social, educational, and economic. These were combined using weights (social criteria were given a weight of three, educational got two, and economic criteria were given a weight of one). This was done for all the Hindu communities. For non-Hindus, the Commission used another set of criteria: all untouchables who converted to other religions and all communities which were identified by their traditional occupations, for which the Hindu counterparts were included in the list of backward classes.

Based on this, the Commission identified 3,743 caste groups as backward, which were 52 per cent of the population (as against 32 per cent identified by the Kalelkar Commission and the roughly 40 per cent from NSS data). The 52 per cent figure was arrived at after subtracting from 100 per cent the share of the SC–ST population, the non-Hindu population based on the 1971 census, and the share of Hindu upper castes extrapolated from the 1931 census. The residual was actually 43.7, to which was added half of the non-Hindu population's share.

The announcement of the implementation of the Mandal Commission Report (MCR) was made in 1990 by the then Prime Minister, V.P. Singh. Under the MCR's recommendation, based on its list as well as the various state lists to identify OBCs, reservations were extended to include an OBC quota of 27 per cent with effect from August 1990, taking the total quota (SC/ST/OBC) to 49.5 per cent. Based on a Supreme Court verdict in the 1963 *Balaji* case, there is a limit on reservations that prohibits reserving a majority of the seats, thus limiting quotas to less than 50 per cent. The figure of 27 per cent for OBCs, therefore, is not in accordance with their share in the population, but is the residual, after accounting for the 22.5 per cent SC–ST quota. Subsequently, the Government of India enacted the National Commission for Backward Classes Act (Act No. 27 of 1993) that set up a National Commission for Backward Classes (NCBC) as a permanent body. Article 340 of the Constitution provides for the appointment of a commission that investigates the conditions of and the difficulties faced by socially and educationally backward classes and to make appropriate recommendations.

The OBC quota is perhaps the only instance of AA in the world where the designated beneficiary category is not counted in the national census. Given that there has been no jati-based census since independence, most of the commissions set up to examine the conditions of the backward classes since then have had to rely on extrapolations from the 1931 census or conduct their own surveys to identify who the backward classes are. The NCBC (as did MCR) set out guidelines for inclusion into the central list of OBCs. These guidelines are listed in the Appendix. As is clear, the NCBC uses a composite set of social, educational, and economic criteria to identify backwardness, with four criteria being considered decisive to the identification of backwardness: 2(e) to 2(h)—castes and communities that are identified with traditional crafts or traditional or hereditary occupations considered to be lowly or undignified, castes associated with 'unclean' or stigmatized occupations, nomadic and semi-nomadic castes and communities, and denotified castes and communities. It re-created the central OBC list afresh, irrespective of whether castes and communities that it designated as backward were included in the MCR list or not. The NCBC functions like a tribunal that decides the validity of the claims made by caste groups for inclusion in the OBC list. It has handled 1,123 claims so far, 675 of which were included in the central list and 448 cases were rejected. Interestingly, it is not always the case that the number of claims that are included are greater than those that are rejected. For example, in Bihar, 12 castes were included as against 22 that were rejected. Odisha had an equal number of rejections and acceptances (45) and for Puducherry, 8 were accepted and 81 rejected.

The announcement of the implementation of MCR was followed by a massive public protest and widespread violent and virulent student agitations across university campuses in the country. Interestingly, despite the disruptions caused by the agitations, public sympathy was fully with the striking students with no evidence of the usual middle–class disdain for and impatience with agitational activities. The police force in Delhi and elsewhere, otherwise not known for its kindness and benevolence, displayed a rare compassion and camaraderie towards the protestors, thus justifying the slogan of the agitating students '*andar ki baat hai, Delhi Police hamare saath hai'* (the inside truth is that Delhi police is with us). Also, while the agitation was caused by the announcement of the MCR and the extension of reservations to OBCs, the protest was against AA in general, with openly derogatory casteist slogans directed against Dalit castes. While V.P. Singh was widely demonized as having created the OBC monster, the problem had been in the public domain independently of, and decades before, V.P. Singh.

### Preferences in Electoral Representation

In addition to provisions related to public employment and education, the Constitution provides reserved seats for SCs and STs in the Lok Sabha (lower house of Parliament) via Article 330 and in Vidhan Sabhas (lower houses of state legislatures) via Article 332. The idea is that historically disadvantaged communities should be provided political space, so that their voice can be heard in elected decision-making bodies and that they are able to influence policies to safeguard their economic interests and fight discrimination. Given the history of electoral reservations discussed earlier in the chapter, it should be noted that this reservation is not in the form of separate electorates, which is, in fact, prohibited by Article 325 (which states that 'no person shall be excluded from any electoral roll on grounds of religion, race, or caste').

In 1993, the 73rd and 74th Constitutional Amendments came into force, after which Article 243 provided for reservation of seats for SCs, STs (in proportion to their population), and for women (33 per cent) in rural and urban local bodies, that is, in the Panchayati Raj Institutions (gram panchayats, block panchayats, and district panchayats) and Nagar Palikas. (Panchayati Raj is a decentralized system of governance, which has the gram panchayat [the village council] as its basic unit. The other tiers are block councils and district councils. Nagar Palikas are urban local bodies or municipal corporations.) Significantly, these amendments ensured that the chairperson's positions at the various levels were reserved as well, which meant that these groups would have a substantive say in decision-making. The logic for these amendments is summed up in the 'Statement of Objects and Reasons' appended to the Constitution as:

> Though the Panchayati Raj Institutions have been in existence for a long time, it has been observed that these institutions have not been able to acquire

the status and dignity of viable and responsive people's bodies due to a number of reasons including absence of regular elections, prolonged supersessions, insufficient representation of weaker sections like Scheduled Castes, Scheduled Tribes and women, inadequate devolution of powers and lack of financial resources.

(This quote is from the Statement of Objects and Reasons to the 73rd amendment; a similar preamble exists for the 74th amendment).

It is significant and noteworthy that insufficient representation of 'weaker' sections is seen as one of the reasons for the lack of vibrancy of local bodies. Also, there is no systematic reservation in local bodies for OBCs, although some states have granted this reservation (discussed in the next chapter).

The beneficiaries of all preferential schemes are SCs, STs, and OBCs; and in the spheres defined by the 73rd and 74th amendments, women are also included. It should be noted that other than for OBCs, the AA policies are group-based, in that all members of the target group are entitled to these benefits, which is one of the key issues in the debate over AA (discussed in Chapter 4). For OBCs, the 'creamy layer' is excluded.

## Reservation for Women

The first Backward Classes Commission recommended that 'all women in India made up a backward class' (Galanter 1984: 169), as they display similar social and economic backwardness as the OBCs, presumably due to the fact that they face similar disabilities and exclusionary structures. However, the question of reservation for women in any sphere was historically never on the agenda. The last decade or so has seen a clear and forceful articulation of the view that AA should be expanded to include women.

The normal process of economic development, on its own, may not increase women's participation in the political sphere. The continued low presence of women in the political spheres of industrialized developed countries is testimony to that. India's actual record is impressive compared to most developed countries: a woman prime minister for 19 years, several women chief ministers, ministers of state, and other important political functionaries at both the central and state government levels. However, as elsewhere in the world, women are under-represented in key decision-making bodies, a feature that has prompted the move to introduce AA.

The 73rd and 74th Amendments, mentioned earlier in this chapter, contained a proposal to reserve 33 per cent of electoral constituencies for women in local self-governments in rural and urban areas. After much debate, the measure was passed in 1993. Three years later, a bill extending such reservation to the parliamentary and state legislative councils was introduced. In 2012, it is still pending in Parliament, mired in huge controversy. While the novelty of the move lies in a version of AA for half of the country's population, the implementation is complicated by the mechanics of working out the overlap with caste-based reservations. However, to believe that the delay is due to mechanics alone would be erroneous. The debate over the passage of the bill has seen a vitriolic upsurge of anti–AA sentiment, in addition to intense anti–women tirades.

Just as major political parties have often revealed an ugly side during this whole debate, a consensus has emerged in the women's movement about the need for AA in the political arena for women, bolstered by the positive experience of panchayat-level reservations (from the implementation of the 73rd and 74th Amendments). There is a belief that a greater representation of women in Parliament will ensure a gender shift in social and economic policies or at least modify the male-dominated and male-biased realm of policymaking. However, there are concerns that some women may be put up as puppets, while the real control would lie with their husbands or other male family members. The counter argument is that even if this happens initially, over time the presence of women in decision-making bodies will help alter both their self-perception and their actual position in society. Indeed, evidence from reservations at the village-council level reveals that gender-based quotas have led to small but significant shifts in policies.

A key issue that has complicated the debate over women's reservation is that of 'quotas-within-quotas'. A section of the political class believes that reserved seats are likely to be dominated by women from relatively upper class/caste backgrounds and, thus to ensure representation of the truly disadvantaged, there should be SC–ST–OBC quotas *within* the women's quota. The other argument used for a quota-within-a-quota is that if caste-based quotas can be used for parliamentary representations in general (that is, for seats that are dominated by men), why should the same principle not be used for seats reserved for women? However, a section of the women's movement is not persuaded and so the issue is not settled yet.

Another issue that comes up in the theoretical literature on gender reservations in politics is that of the appropriate level at which seats should be reserved for women: should political parties reserve seats for women, that is, field more women candidates, or should more constituencies be reserved for women? The question that the literature examines is which of these is more likely to increase representation of women in elected bodies. In India, at the practical level, the quota-within-quotas is currently the real debate.

# 3

# Implementation of Affirmative Action Provisions

This chapter takes stock of the state of implementation of affirmative action (AA) measures outlined in the previous chapter. Overall, the implementation of Scheduled Caste (SC) and Scheduled Tribe (ST) quotas has improved in all spheres, but despite safeguards it remains uneven. At the outset, it is important to place the lackadaisical implementation of quotas in some perspective. Most government schemes in India are characterized by poor implementation. Consider, for instance, something as straightforward and non-controversial as income tax or, more generally, the various taxes which citizens are supposed to pay to the government. The rates are clearly announced, eligibility is well-defined, and the principle that citizens should pay taxes is not disputed, even though there might be a dispute over rates. However, while groups continue to lobby for lowering rates or exemptions, while a given rate is in operation, taxes are supposed to be paid according to the given rate. Yet, a 2010 study by the Comptroller and Auditor General of India found rampant tax evasion to the extent of 50 per cent in half of the 23 states where tax audits were carried out (http://articles.timesofindia.indiatimes.com/2010-07-25/india-business/28320914_1_tax-evasion-tax-exemptions-indirect-tax-regime). This evasion is not only with respect to income tax. The study found that in three states, taking advantage of a special scheme, manufacturers collected huge amounts (Rs 6,400 crore), but had not remitted tax in four years, with the Reliance group of companies accounting for more than 90 per cent of this amount. Here the identity of the evader is known clearly. Anyone who has tried to buy or sell property in India knows very well that it is virtually impossible to conduct a transaction without the mandatory 'black' component (that is, part of the payment in cash which is unaccounted for). One could go on with examples of tax evasion or indeed of other schemes that are characterized by poor implementation. Very few will argue that given poor tax recovery, the *principle* of taxation has been a failure and thus should be abandoned; yet for schemes such as AA, the poor or uneven implementation is routinely used to justify a removal of the policy.

When we discuss uneven or poor implementation of the reservation policy, a critical part of the picture is the lack of political will on the part of those who are entrusted with its implementation. All political parties pay lip-service to the reservation agenda, but predominant interests in bureaucracies, and overall in the state machinery, prevent adequate implementation. Given that there is no formal systematic monitoring of implementation, it remains subject to the vagaries of political will and an overall lackadaisical attitude. This suggests that AA has to be viewed as a dynamic policy, which should be subject to regular and detailed review based on feedback from below, such that weaknesses in implementation can be highlighted and steps can be taken to make the policy more effective. The last chapter discusses how the policy could be made more dynamic, instead of its current state, where the announcement of quotas is seen as the beginning and end of AA.

# Implementation of Quotas in
# Government Jobs

Posts are reserved for SCs, STs, and Other Backward Classes (OBCs) in all groups of posts in the case of direct recruitment. When the recruitment is done at the national level by open competition (for example, Union Public Service Commission) reservation for the three groups is 15, 7.5, and 27 per cent, respectively. However, if the recruitment is not through open competition, the quotas are 16.6, 7.5, and 25.84 per cent, respectively. In the case of direct recruitment to Category C and D jobs, which mainly attract local applicants, the percentage of reserved seats is fixed in proportion to the SC–ST population in the given state, and for OBCs, the quota is fixed such that it does not exceed 27 per cent. Reservation in promotions is available only for SCs–STs, not for OBCs. In the public sector, jobs are classified into four types, distinguished by selection requirements and income: Class I (or Group A); Class II (or Group B); Class III (or Group C); and Class IV (or Group D). Class I, which is the highest paid, includes officers of the Indian Administrative Service (IAS); Indian Foreign

Service (IFS); Indian Police Service (IPS); and related central-government services. Class II employees are officers of the state civil-service cadre. Both Class I and II jobs are filled through competitive examinations and interviews. Class III and IV (or Groups C and D) jobs include all the low-skill, low-qualification jobs, which are also low-income jobs and form the majority of government jobs. Of the central-government jobs, 94 per cent are Class III and IV jobs.

The implementation of quotas has improved over time, though it is far from perfect and displays variations by category of jobs. For instance, in the topmost categories of officers, Group A or Class I jobs, between 1964 and 1984, the share of SCs increased from 1.6 to only 7 per cent, as compared to their share in the population which was roughly 16 per cent. However, the 1994 to 2004 phase saw a sharper increase, such that in 2004, their share was 12.2 per cent. (The corresponding shares for STs were 0.3 and 1.7, which went to 4.1 in 2004, as against a population share of around 7 per cent.) Sheth (2004) argues that this reflects the aftermath of the Mandal phase, which created the space for a greater assertion of Dalit or low-caste activism, one consequence of which was better implementation of quotas. Interestingly, in 2004, only 4 per cent of Group A officers were OBCs, which is the same proportion as the STs.

Before the 1990s, for years quotas remained unful-filled, revealing a picture quite like Delhi University discussed later in the chapter. This can be attributed to 'indifference/hostility on the part of the appoint-ing authorities, insufficient publicization of vacancies and the sheer expense of application' (Galanter 1984: 97). At the higher levels or promotion stages, formal and informal procedures operated to keep out the SCs, such as ad hoc and temporary positions, elimination through personal evaluation procedures like inter-views, personality tests, and unfair adverse entries in confidential records (Guhan 2001: 213).

As one goes down the hierarchy, the representation of SCs–STs increases, with as many as 80 per cent of the cleaners being SCs in 2007. Overall, the Group D category has always had more SCs than their share in the population, even excluding sweepers. This sug-gests that within the government, all the low-paid and low-skill jobs are dominated by SCs. Thus, to repeat a point made in Chapter 1, the link between caste and occupation might be broken for some castes, but for

Dalits, the link between caste and status, and in many cases, the more direct link between caste and occupation persists (seen especially in the case of scavengers and sweepers). Sahoo (2009) reports on figures for the implementation of quotas separately for central-government services, central public sector units, and central civil service jobs and the picture is more or less the same, with more rapid implementation in the post-Mandal phase.

This overall picture hides a lot of variation in specific institutions. Some case studies can provide a starker picture of the ground realities in implementation of reservations. Teachers in Delhi University, a premier university in the country, have bitterly opposed the introduction of quotas even though it is a constitutional provision. As a result, reservations were introduced as late as 1996. At that time, out of the 700 teachers in postgraduate departments, 7 were SCs and 2 were STs. Out of the 4,512 teachers in university affiliated undergraduate colleges, 11 were SCs and none were STs (Xaxa 2002). The picture in the non-teaching posts conforms to the overall pattern in other government jobs: the higher the representation of SCs/STs, the lower paying the job. Xaxa's (2002) figures for 1998–9 show that whereas only 3 per cent of Group A jobs were filled by SCs/STs combined, the corresponding proportions for Groups B, C, and D were 7.4, 13, and 29 per cent, respectively. Menial jobs (cleaners, sweepers, and so on) are often performed almost exclusively by Dalits, in particular those jatis whose traditional occupation was cleaning/scavenging. In all the opposition to AA, there is never any protest against *over-representation* of low castes in low-paying jobs. In other words, as long as Dalits do not compete in traditional upper-caste bastions or 'stay where they belong', it is obviously considered acceptable. In 2006, Delhi University took some symbolic steps to redress these gaps. It set up an Equal Opportunity Cell, which is mainly geared towards providing equal opportunity of employment and physical access to the differently abled, but also states in its list of objectives 'the implementation of affirmative action towards SC, ST, OBC'. However, its mission statement and list of activities for the last three years of its existence is mainly geared towards the inclusion of physically handicapped and differently abled individuals, which is welcome, but its activities do not indicate any specific attempts to ensure enforcement of affirmative action.

This picture of Delhi University is unfortunately not unique. Sahoo (2009: 52–3) quotes figures from the annual reports of the National Commission for Scheduled Castes and Scheduled Tribes (NCSC&ST). The 1994 report reveals that there were 2 SCs out of a total of 1,155 professors in central universities (that is, 0.2 per cent). Among readers (associate professors), there were 6 out of a total of 1,774. The position of STs was even worse, as they were heavily under-represented in all teaching positions, including in the north-east, where STs have a substantial presence in the population. The 2001 NCSC&ST report reveals that in the 256 universities and about 11,000 colleges funded by the UGC, with 3.42 lakh teaching positions, SCs and STs comprised only 2 per cent and about 75,000 reserved teaching positions were vacant. The figures for Delhi University from this report reveal that during 1999–2001, there were 15 teachers who were SCs (3 professors [0.3 per cent], 2 readers [1 per cent], and 9 lecturers [6.4 per cent]) and 3 teachers who were STs (1 professor [0.03 per cent], no readers, and 2 lecturers [1.4 per cent]).

Data on the representation of SCs–STs in non-reserved public institutions is also revealing. For instance, in the elite Indian Institute of Technology (IIT), reservation is provided only at the lecturer or assistant professor levels. The NCSC&ST report for 2001 states that only three lecturers were from SCs/STs and these individuals had got their jobs without availing of the quota, or through 'open' selection. Similarly, in government-aided private management schools, SCs and STs accounted for 10 per cent, whereas in government schools, teachers from these sections comprised 17.6 per cent of the total (Sahoo 2009: 54).

Representation in specialized jobs with no reservation also reveals under-representation of individuals from SC/ST communities. For instance, only 20 of the 610 High Court judges were SC (less than 3 per cent) in 1997–8 (Sahoo 2009: 54). Till 1998, there was no single ST judge. Similarly, SC representation among officers in the defence forces was 7.2 per cent in 2000, whereas for STs it was 2.4 per cent. These shares have been fairly stagnant since 1990. This suggests that in the absence of reservations, the shares of SCs–STs are likely to be low in the higher categories—probably even lower than their existing share.

The representation of OBCs in public sector units also shows a mixed picture. In 2005, they were under-represented in Groups A and B (6.3 and 8.4 per cent, respectively), but they were 17 and 22.6 per cent in Groups C and D, respectively, with a total of 15.5 per cent.

## Implementation of Quotas in Higher Education

Quotas in higher education are similar to job quotas: 15 per cent seats are reserved for SCs and 7.4 per cent for STs in undergraduate and postgraduate courses of all kinds—general, technical, medical, and other professional courses. These quotas are also applicable in IITs, Indian Institutes of Management (IIMs), Regional Engineering Colleges, and central universities. In 2006, via the 93rd Constitutional Amendment, and amidst a great deal of furore, a 27 per cent mandatory quota for OBCs was introduced in higher educational institutions. However, as we have seen earlier, OBC quotas existed in different states for several decades prior to this announcement. In one sense, this OBC quota is an additional requirement mainly for central educational institutions since a large number state-level educational colleges and universities already had an OBC quota.

Access to education by caste can be, and has been, analysed at various levels—literacy rates, quality of education, primary-to-middle school transition, and evidence of discrimination inside schools. From the strict point of view of implementation of AA, however, we need to focus on a few key statistics, while recognizing that the problem of equitable access and representation across caste groups in the sphere of education is far too large and far too complex to be captured through these few numbers.

A common measure for access to higher education is generally the enrolment ratio in higher education. Three alternative methods are used to estimate enrolment: gross enrolment ratio (GER), net enrolment ratio (NER), and enrolment of eligible ratio (EER). These enrolment measures can be applied to any level of education, and at the higher education level, GER measures the access level by taking the ratio of persons in all age groups enrolled in various programmes to the total population in the age group 18 to 23 years. The NER measures the level of enrolment for age-specific groups—those in the age group of 18 to 23 years, while EER measures the level of enrolment of those who have completed higher-secondary-level education.

Overall, GER for higher education, which rose from 0.7 per cent in 1950–1, to 1.4 per cent in 1960–1, and to 8 per cent in early 2000, is still very low (about 10 per cent) compared to the world average of 23.2 per cent, and an average of 54.6 per cent for developed countries, 36.3 per cent for countries in transition, and 11.3 per cent for developing countries. The existing EER of roughly 60 per cent indicates that 40 per cent of the students who complete their higher secondary programmes do not go in for higher education.

Within this picture of low overall GER, there is substantial variation by caste and gender. Thus, data from NSS for 2004–5 reveals that only 9.7 per cent of rural SC men and 3.5 per cent of rural SC women in the age group 20–24 years were enrolled in higher educational institutions, as compared to 14.9 and 6 per cent of rural 'Other' men and women, respectively. The corresponding figures for rural STs were 8.6 and 5.2 per cent and for OBCs, they were 11 and 4.1, respectively (Sahoo 2009). The major fault lines across which we see marked differences in enrolment rates are rural–urban—in all caste groups, urban participation rates are consistently higher than rural and these gaps have widened over time; gender—in all the caste groups, men had greater representation in higher education than women; and by age groups—across all caste groups, access at the undergraduate level was significantly higher than at the postgraduate level.

The Delhi University study cited earlier (Xaxa 2002) confirms this national picture. It shows that in 1999–2000, of all the undergraduate students, only 8.6 per cent were SCs (with a quota of 15 per cent) and 1.8 per cent were STs (quota of 7 per cent). Of the postgraduate students, 5.5 per cent were SCs and 2 per cent were STs (with actual quotas the same as those at the undergraduate level).

The Selected Educational Statistics (SES), brought out by the Ministry of Human Resource and Development, reveal inter-caste differences in patterns of enrolment in different courses. According to the SES for 2004–5, the proportion of SCs in higher education (18–24 years) was 7 per cent and that for STs was 5 per cent. Between 1966–7 and 2004–5, the proportions of SC and ST students enrolled in engineering, technology, medicine, and commerce degrees—the more specialized and sought-after courses—increased, but was well short of the mandated quotas. These groups continued to have higher representation (albeit less than the quota) in liberal arts and BA programmes, rather than in specialized courses at the undergraduate level or in all courses at the postgraduate level, which were overwhelmingly dominated by 'Others' (between 80 to 90 per cent of the students in the latter courses were non-SCs–STs).

There is substantial inter-state variation in the implementation of quotas in higher education. Sahoo (2009: 74) reports that SCs' access to higher education was worse in states which had a high concentration of the SC population, for example, Punjab and Bihar. In general, SC participation rates in the southern states were better than those in the northern and north-western states. For STs, participation rates in the tribal dominated north–eastern states were significantly higher than in states with a high concentration of tribals such as Odisha, where the ST participation rate was 0.8 per cent, Madhya Pradesh (0.4), Chhattisgarh (1.5), and Jharkhand (2.2).

Participation rates for OBCs were distinctly greater than for SCs and STs. For Hindu OBCs, these were about 26 per cent among the total graduates in the 20–30 years age group and about 28 per cent among the currently studying population, according to the

NSS 2004–5 data. These are close to the currently mandated quota.

SC–ST quotas in premier institutions such as IITs remain incompletely filled. Thus, in 2005–6, in all IITs combined, there were 12 per cent SC and 4 per cent ST students. The nature of the selection process in the IITs is more difficult. SC and ST candidates have to appear for the joint entrance examination, and all those who score more than two-thirds the marks of the last non-reserved candidate are admitted directly. Those who score less than this but pass the exam, are given a year-long preparatory course, at the end of which they have to appear for an examination. If they clear this examination, they are then admitted for a regular course in IIT. There is no relaxation in the pass marks, but SC–ST students get a longer time span to complete their degree. Prima facie, this confirms the belief that due to past disadvantages, including poorer quality of school education, SC–ST students might not be suited for technically demanding courses such as those offered by the IITs. However, the next chapter considers this 'mismatch' hypothesis and offers evidence from studies in India which have rigorously deconstructed this hypothesis.

# Political Reservations

The one arena in which quotas have been implemented completely is the sphere of political reservations. Originally, reservations in the elected sphere were provided for a period of 10 years (under Article 334), but this was extended, each time by another 10 years. Whether these reservations should exist in perpetuity is an important question, which is discussed in Chapter 4 as a part of the debates around AA.

Currently, there are 79 (15 per cent) and 41 (8.2 per cent) seats in the Lok Sabha and 540 and 282 seats in the Vidhan Sabhas for SCs and STs, respectively (Sahoo 2009: 86). In principle, members of both these groups are free to contest from other, non-reserved seats. However, since the first general elections in 1952, SC–ST elected representatives have virtually no presence in these two elected bodies outside of the reserved seats. This suggests that if reservations had not been in existence, the probability that these groups would have the representation they currently have would be very low. If the presence of SC–ST legislators and members of Parliament (MPs) is taken as a measure of political clout, then there is no evidence of an *increase* in their political clout. If anything, there is a marginal decline: in 1952, SCs won 76 seats in the Lok Sabha against the 72 seats reserved for them, which means they won 4 non-reserved seats. In 2004, SCs won only the 79 seats reserved for them, and none from the non-reserved seats. For STs, the picture is fairly similar; the only election where they won on more seats than were reserved for them was in 1998 (won 49 as against 41 reserved). In 2004, they won only the 41 reserved seats (Sahoo 2009: 88).

The picture in the local bodies is different, underscoring the importance of the 73rd and 74th Amendments in achieving a radical transformation in political representation of the marginalized groups. In the early 1960s, when there were no reservations, local bodies in West Bengal with a total of 1,081 members had only 41 SC members (3.8 per cent) and 16 ST members (1.5 per cent). Among the 66 presidents and chairmen, there were 3 SC members and 1 ST members. This was at a time when 19.84 per cent of the population of West Bengal was SC, and 5.91 per cent was ST. Similarly, in Gujarat, only 35 (0.5 per cent) of the 6,863 sarpanches were SC (Galanter 1984: 50–1).

Now, thanks to reservations in local bodies, SC–ST presence in the lower levels of governance has increased substantially, often going beyond the mandated reservations. For instance, in Odisha, Chhattisgarh, Madhya Pradesh, and Rajasthan, SCs/STs have between 30–40 per cent representation at the gram-panchayat level. Even at the level of the district panchayats, there are 14 per cent SCs and 9 per cent STs, which together is marginally greater than their share in the population (Sahoo 2009: 88).

Jaffrelot (2003) argues that the rise of Dalit parties such as the Bahujan Samaj Party in Uttar Pradesh and, overall, the growing recognition of SCs in the Indian political system found expression in the election of the first Dalit president of the country, K.R. Narayanan from Kerala. Even though he was widely respected for his intelligence, statesmanship, and integrity, even he could not escape jibes on account of his untouchable origin, with particular derogatory references to the traditional occupation of the caste he belonged to.

## Political Representation of OBCs

As noted in the previous chapter, there is no political reservation for OBCs at the national level, although some state governments (for example, Uttar Pradesh, Karnataka, and Tamil Nadu) have reserved seats for OBCs at the level of local self-government. Unlike in the case of SCs–STs, there is very little hard data on the proportion of elected representatives who are OBCs at the various levels of government. However, the big difference between SCs–STs, on the one hand, and OBCs, on the other, is that the last two decades have seen a visible increase in the political clout of OBC politicians and political formations, not uniformly across all regions of India but in a large enough number of pockets.

The southern parts of the country, particularly Tamil Nadu and Karnataka, have had a long history of backward class mobilization as a result of the anti-Brahmin movements since the late nineteenth century. The rise of OBC politicians and political clout continued after independence. In Tamil Nadu, for instance, the two largest political parties, the Dravida Munnetra Kazhagam (DMK) and the All India Anna Dravida Munnetra Kazhagam (AIADMK) are largely OBC-backed parties. Karnataka has seen a distinct rise of OBC dominance in politics since the 1960s, which resulted in Devraj Urs becoming the Chief Minister of the state in 1972. Deve Gowda, another prominent OBC leader from the state became the Prime Minister of the country in 1998 heading a non-Congress, non-BJP (Bharatiya Janata Party) coalition government. Maharashtra and Gujarat in the western part of the country have seen a similar rise of OBC politicians, including the current Chief Minister of Gujarat, Narendra Modi. Maharashtra has seen the dominance of OBC politicians in general, and Maratha politicians in particular, since independence. Some of the Maratha leaders, well-known at the national level, are Yashwant Rao Chavan, Sharad Pawar, and Vasantdada Patil, among others. Vasant Rao Naik is a prominent OBC leader from the Vanjara community.

In the north, the increase in political clout of the OBCs and their marked political assertion started only around the 1970s. Ram Manohar Lohia's Samyukta Socialist Party was opposed to reservations in education for SCs but clearly favoured increased political representation for the OBCs, and quotas for 'backwards' as discussed in the previous chapter. In addition, Charan Singh was championing *kisan* (peasants) interests, mainly to highlight the interests of his own caste, the Jats, but the larger category of kisans also included other low castes. Charan Singh and the socialists joined hands and formed the first Janata government in 1977, which is considered as the first landmark event in the rise of lower castes in politics (the second landmark being the second Janata government and the implementation of the Mandal Commission Report). As a result of the political ascendancy of the intermediate and backward castes, the upper castes (Brahmins and Thakurs), who had near-total control of the decision-making institutions in the Hindi speaking belt, were down to less than 50 per cent in 1977 (Jaffrelot 2003). Among MPs from the Hindi heartland, the OBC strength went up from 11 per cent in 1984 to 25 per cent in 1996 (and this share is greater if the intermediate castes are included). Over the same period, the share of upper-caste MPs declined from 47 to 35 per cent (Ibid.). The politics of Uttar Pradesh and Bihar has especially been dominated by Yadavs as a caste group; the political importance of Lalu Prasad Yadav and Sharad Yadav from Bihar and Mulayam Singh Yadav from Uttar Pradesh cannot be overemphasized. The rise of OBCs in the Hindi belt has not been confined to any particular party. As Jaffrelot (2003) puts it: 'whatever the party in office, the chief ministers have mostly been OBC leaders in the Hindi belt—the crucible of the ongoing silent revolution—over the last ten years, a situation which stands in stark contrast with the one which prevailed before'.

The rise of the OBCs as a potent political force, dominating a whole spectrum of political parties, has, in the main, happened without reservations, again suggesting that stigmatization on account of their untouchable status imparts a particular disadvantage to the SCs, which includes, but goes beyond, the economic and social marginalization which the OBCs face.

## Political Representation of Women

Despite the presence of some prominent women leaders in the national parties, participation of women in general elections is far from optimal. In the 2009 Lok Sabha elections, for a total of 543 seats, the national parties put up a combined total of 134 women candidates, 43 of these won, representing a total of 6 per cent of the votes polled. An additional 27 women contested from state parties, out of which 15 got elected, representing 2 per cent of the votes polled in the state. This was despite the fact that at the national level, 48 per cent of voters were women, and 47 per cent of the votes polled were cast by women (figures from the Election Commission of India, 2009 General Elections). In other words, women's participation in the electoral process as voters is vigorous and strong; the problem lies with the political parties, or the political class, which are reluctant to field women candidates. Political reservations for women at the level of the Lok Sabha and Vidhan Sabhas will, of course, increase representation of women. These figures reveal why political parties are reluctant to endorse reservations for women: left to decide for themselves, they would rather keep women in a minority.

On the whole, then the message is clear: representation of disadvantaged groups is very low in spheres where there is no reservation, and where there is reservation, it is unevenly implemented.

## State-level Variations in Quotas

As the preceding discussion illustrates, the extent of quotas in different regions varied substantially under colonial rule. This heterogeneity continues in post-independence India as well, where the present-day states are combinations of erstwhile British territories as well as princely states. This section discusses some important state-level differences in reservation policies.

### *Karnataka*

Present-day Karnataka was created in 1956 by integrating Kannada-speaking areas of the former Hyderabad, Bombay, and Madras provinces with the princely state of Mysore. As discussed previously, these regions were among the first to implement caste and community based quotas in the early twentieth century, some parts had a rudimentary quota system dating back to the late nineteenth century. The first Backward Classes Committee was appointed in 1918 under the chairmanship of Sir Leslie Miller, the Chief Judge of the Mysore Chief Court, which recommended specific caste quotas. These were implemented immediately and continued even after independence until 1956. After the formation of the new state, it was necessary to redefine reservation, in view of the inclusion of new territories in the state. The Karnataka government's attempt to extend reservations using the same criteria as the one used in princely Mysore was struck down twice, first by the Mysore High Court in 1958 and then by the Supreme Court in 1959. The second Backward Classes Committee, under the chairmanship of Nagana Gowda was set up in 1960. The recommendations of this committee were struck down by the Supreme Court in the landmark *Balaji v. Mysore* case, citing the use of caste as the sole criterion for backwardness and for recommending reservations greater than 50 per cent.

This was followed by two other commissions called the First and the Second Backward Classes *Commissions* (to distinguish them from the two earlier committees). While the detailed history of these bodies is chequered and their recommendations marked by contestation about which jatis deserve reservations (see Thimmaiah 1997 for details), the point to note is that the absence of jati-wise data makes it very difficult to verify claims and counter-claims. For instance, the Gowda Committee used the 1931 estimates of certain jatis and used the rate of growth between 1931 and 1941 to guess-estimate population shares in 1960, which proved to be controversial. The Second Backward Classes Commission (1983) conducted a household census, the first after independence, to get a more accurate picture of the caste composition. However, their estimates too were rejected as inaccurate on the grounds that the census was not comprehensive, a charge accepted by the Commission. However, the extent of underestimation by the Commission was again disputed; the estimates ranged from the Commission's own admission of 7 per cent to 30 per cent.

The main challenge in Karnataka, illustrated by the *Balaji* case, was to reduce pre-existing levels of quotas to under 50 per cent. Keeping existing quotas (through government amendments) would have meant repeated litigation by non-targeted groups and reducing the coverage of quotas would have upset the existing political configuration of various groups. The compromise was to use income and occupation as eligibility criteria, rather than caste. Under this system, all those earning Rs 1,200 or less per year with the following occupations: 'cultivator, artisan, petty businessman, inferior service, or other occupation involving manual labour': were considered backward and 30 per cent seats were reserved for them (Galanter 1984: 192–3). However, with this new policy the dominant groups of Brahmins, Lingayats, and Vokkaligas in society (the latter two deemed backward under some commissions and not under others) monopolized the reserved positions, often with false income certificates (Parikh 1997: 163). Galanter argues that while the popular reading of *Balaji* believes that it outlawed caste as a basis for determining backwardness, in reality, it allowed for caste as a permissible criterion, but not a mandatory one. That, of course, begs the essential question which continues to haunt these debates, not just in Karnataka but in the rest of the country: what set of criteria would be optimal to determine backwardness?

### Bihar

This question is particularly pertinent in Bihar, one of India's poorest states, which has all the elements included in the definition of backwardness: in addition to caste and tribal status, there is poverty, low educational levels, and geographical remoteness. Based on an estimate which projects the 1931 proportions, the four high castes—Brahmins, Rajputs, Bhumihars, and Kayasthas—constituted 13 per cent of the state population. The backward castes were estimated to be 52 per cent of the population, with the Yadavas being the single largest caste at 11 per cent. The next largest backward caste constituted the Kurmis at 4 per cent of the population (Sachchidananda 1997: 163). Yadavs, Kurmis, Koeris, and 31 other castes constituted the advanced sections of the backward castes and 94 other communities, including some Muslim communities, were designated as 'extremely backward'.

The SC–ST list for Bihar was promulgated through a Presidential order in 1950. The Kaka Kalelkar Commission (discussed in the previous chapter) listed 127 castes, both Hindu and Muslim, constituting 31.1 per cent of the state's population, as 'backward'. However, the report of this Commission was rejected, for reasons discussed earlier, and the state government appointed a Backward Classes Commission under the chairmanship of Shri Mungeri Lal in December 1971. The report of this Commission identified 128 backward communities across Hindus, Muslims, and Christians and found significant under-representation of SCs–STs as well as of these communities at various levels of government service. Debates in Bihar over which communities are truly backward are very similar to debates in other states.

However, in Bihar, the quota debates have entered another dimension. In 2007, the SCs were further stratified into a category of 'Maha Dalit' (more Dalit than other Dalits), the backward among the SCs. Bihar is not the only state to have done this sub-classification. Punjab, Haryana, and Andhra Pradesh have created similar categories. Initially, 18 of the 23 SCs were identified as Maha Dalits; over time, however, more castes have been added to this category, as a result of which the distinction between the overall SC category and the Maha Dalits has been shrinking. This move has generated a mixed response even from within the Dalit community, with Ram Vilas Paswan, a prominent Dalit politician from the state opposing the move as he believed it tried to 'sow the seeds of divisiveness among the Dalit fraternity' (*The Hindu,* 5 April 2010).

One can similarly examine other state stories: in Rajasthan, Gujjars asked for a 5 per cent quota and asked to be classified as an ST. The most powerful tribal group in Rajasthan, the Meenas, contested their claim and threatened to launch an agitation if the Gujjars were given an ST status. There are several such state-specific controversies. In each one, we find a similar refrain: the debate is over which groups are truly disadvantaged or backward. Is there a set of unambiguous criteria which could be used to get answers to this question? It turns out that the debates are long-standing, very complex, and extremely difficult to unravel in the light of non-existent data. The dilemma, mentioned in Chapter 1, whether 'to count or not to count' is indeed pertinent, especially in view of the experiences of various commissions whose attempts to count or estimate backwardness were rejected on grounds of inadequate rigour. The complexities and difficulties of counting notwithstanding, *not counting* definitely does not get us any closer to understanding the reality of backwardness.

# 4

# The Quota Debates

The uneven implementation of quotas over six decades of national-level affirmative action (AA), not counting the pre-independence provisions, has led several to question the utility of quotas. Given the state of implementation, should we strive for better implementation or abolish quotas altogether? While no political party officially raises this demand, there are strong voices among the intelligentsia, the media, and from various middle-class groups demanding the abolition of quotas. The logical way to approach this question would be to examine evidence from informed studies of the AA programme in its current state of implementation, which will enable us to separate the costs of the AA programme arising from improper implementation and costs (if any) that are being imposed *because of* quotas.

Unfortunately, debates on AA have generated more heat than light. At the outset, we should note that debates over AA can be classified into two basic types: one set of debates consists of controversies surrounding inclusion and exclusion of specific groups into the programme and over the extent of quotas (what percentage of seats should be reserved). The previous chapter referred to some of these debates, and there are several others. However, the basic question underlying these controversies is the same. The second set of debates is over the efficacy and purpose of AA—about the principle criteria used to identify beneficiaries and about the costs versus benefits of the programme. This chapter focuses on the latter set of debates.

If the basic objection to quotas or AA could be summed up in one word, it would be injustice. Quotas are widely seen as unfair, and are condemned for punishing innocent upper castes for the damage done in the past, for reinforcing caste lines rather than striving for a caste-free society, and for exempting Dalits from the rigours of market competition. Critics argue that reservations replace one form of discrimination (against Dalits) with another, equally pernicious form (against non-quota students or workers).

These perspectives are, however, unconvincing from the viewpoint of the Dalits, who argue that the most powerful special privileges actually accrue to high-caste Hindus who can tap into exclusive social networks, bank on the cultural capital their families bequeath to them, or pay the bribes that are demanded by employers for access to jobs.

A study of the transition from college-to-work (Deshpande and Newman 2007) documents several upper-caste and Dalit voices, both against and in favour of reservations. There is a view, especially among the upper castes, that quotas are benefiting a generation whose parents have already moved up in the social structure and have been able to give them benefits denied to other, much poorer, and more remote young people. Second, there is a belief that unqualified students are displacing highly qualified students in the race to the top of the educational heap. Many who share this view argue strenuously that the application of reservations will destroy the competitiveness of the Indian economy and drive away foreign investors because of the privileges ensured by reservation. Hence they fuse personal exclusion with a national downfall in the making.

Other critics of reservations argue that the policy may indeed be positive—in the sense that it redresses tremendous inequities—but ends up being a colossal waste because the high drop-out rates that Scheduled Caste (SC) and Scheduled Tribe (ST) students suffer from negates their impact. These places could have been taken by general category students who would complete their demanding courses, but instead are being taken by people who had almost no chance by virtue of poor preparation.

However, for Dalits, AA in higher education not only enables their ascent in the university world, it literally enables them to 'open their mouths', meaning speak their minds and 'go to the centre of society', where they can 'meet other people ... and get a platform' (Deshpande and Newman 2007). The silence imposed by marginality, caste prejudice (enforced by atrocities, especially in rural areas), and poverty is broken by introducing these Dalit students to another world and a different future. They are well aware that without this social policy intervention, they could have remained stuck in a life that would never provide the kind of options they see before them now. These opportunities are critical not only because they promote social mobility, but because reservations literally rescue Dalits from a lifetime of exploitation at the hands of landlords, abusive employers, and neighbours who can turn on them without provocation and remind them forcefully of their subordinate status. Legal guarantees in the form of anti-atrocity regulations mean nothing in the context of weak enforcement.

For those aware of the history of the political struggle that resulted in the creation of the quota system, reservation is seen as a noble commitment to equality, struck by the hero of the Dalit social movement, B.R. Ambedkar. This history is sacred to Dalit students, for it represents the first victory in a long and unfinished struggle for human rights and full equality, a campaign that remains as vital as ever as a source of inspiration for the poor and excluded. For Dalit students, the reservations policy is nothing more than a form of social engineering designed to address centuries of oppression and discrimination, extreme inequities in the distribution of educational opportunities, and the formation of a huge class of Indian citizens who are not equipped to compete without this assistance. These are not matters of history. Dalits cite countless examples from their own experience where they have been interrogated about their caste identities, castigated by prospective employers for their support of reservations, subjected to harassment or disrespect, and denied jobs (as far as they know) solely on account of their caste background. As long as this injustice persists, they argue, reservations will be needed. The policy levels the playing field at the vital choke points of social mobility. They are not special privileges that unfairly advantage; they are compensation for historic and contemporary injustices that creates some measure of equality in outcomes.

Dalits from remote areas see themselves as doubly disadvantaged, by caste bias and by poverty. In comparison to Dalits from civil service families, it is harder for poor, rural Dalits to attend secondary school in the first place, since their families need their labour and the school fees and costs for books or boarding are prohibitive. They struggle out of rural areas burdened by social isolation, ill-equipped in terms of cultural capital to navigate an urban megalopolis like Delhi, and lack social networks that the more privileged caste-mates rely on. The cosmopolitan panache and the confidence which comes with it is vital to make a good impression on the selectors in a job interview, and Dalit students feel disadvantaged in these respects as compared to their upper-caste and upper-class peers. This poses yet another barrier to them as they try to move into the labour market. Although most of the reservation students recognized that their fluency in English—an important skill for success in higher education and later in professional employment—is weak relative to high-caste students, those of rural origin see themselves as even farther behind in this regard.

For the poorer Dalit students, the provision of a quota in admissions has made the difference between a life of poverty and a life of possibility. Yet the financial hardships they face threaten to derail their studies, or put them at a disadvantage when out of necessity they have to search for work during their university years. Facing additional academic burdens—often the need for remedial education to come up to par—while bearing additional responsibility is a recipe for failure, and many reserved category students fail to graduate for these reasons. Students from a more comfortable background face fewer challenges and, in the view of their poorer counterparts, may even come to take reservation seats for granted, as something of a birth right, which the poorer Dalit students view as a matter of concern.

It would be incorrect to portray all upper castes as unanimously against reservations. There are upper castes, both in universities and outside, for whom equality is a high principle and the barriers to achieving it for historically oppressed people clear enough. They embrace the purpose of reservation and see in it the possibilities for upward mobility. Among these supporters, there are differences of opinion nonetheless about the effectiveness of reservations for the same reason that critics voice: high drop-out rates. The lesson to be learned for these more progressive voices, though, is not to abandon reservations, but redouble efforts to address educational inequality at much younger ages. Without a massive commitment to improving primary-school education, they argue, we cannot really expect reservations to succeed. If not for reasons of equity, then for reasons of efficiency, differential investment is required.

The debates on AA have not only been confined to the streets and in op-ed columns. There is a vast body of litigation on issues arising from AA which has influenced the exact manner of its implementation.

Galanter (1984) presents the complex and detailed history of legal interpretations of constitutional provisions. Essentially, three major constitutional issues have arisen in the court cases over AA.

## How Many Places Ought to Be Reserved?

The Constitution does not explicitly provide any maximum or a limit on the extent of preferences. However, since preferences take the form of quotas, there has always been an implicit discussion in terms of limits to quotas. Ambedkar was of the view that reservations ought to be limited to a minority and in fact suggested that 70 per cent of the posts fell outside the purview of Article 16(4). Ambedkar also envisaged a judicial review of the extent of reservations, although the actual text of the Article does not contain anything which suggests this.

In the landmark case of *Balaji v. State of Mysore*, the Supreme Court suggested a ceiling of 50 per cent, with the logic that 'speaking generally and in a broad way, a special provision should be less than 50 per cent … and how much less than 50 per cent would depend upon the relevant prevailing circumstances in each case' (Galanter 1984: 401). It interpreted the quota not as a special benefit conferred upon some groups, but as a measure which would promote the interests of the entire society by promoting the interests of its weakest elements. Hence, the idea was that the promotion of the most backward has to be interwoven with the utilization of the full pool of national talent. The way to balance these two considerations would be to keep quotas at less than 50 per cent. In actual fact, the 50 per cent limit has been seen as a flat maximum, a fixed ceiling, with the 'less than' provision being ignored in most cases. In another important case, *Devadasan v. Union of India*, a majority of the judges found that any quota above the 50 per cent rule would be 'unconstitutional'.

The question of a limit on quotas boils down to figuring out a number which will strike a 'reasonable balance' (Galanter 1984: 404) between the claims of the beneficiary groups and those of other communities. Galanter (1984) points out an inherent contradiction in the Supreme Court verdict which says that 'the reservation for backward communities should not be so excessive as to create a monopoly or unduly disturb the legitimate claim of other communities'. As he explains it, the point is that other communities have no constitutional claims as *communities* ... the only 'claim' that other communities have is the right to compete in an open merit competition as individuals. There is an inherent tension here and seen in this way, as Galanter argues, 50 per cent is a mechanical rule. It will 'not resolve the tension between the right of all to open merit competition and the right of some to merit selection' (Ibid.: 406). More important, whether the probability of selection for individuals from the general population gets adversely affected by reservations, and to what extent, is not only a function of the proportion of seats reserved (x or y per cent) but is equally a function of the total number of seats, the total (absolute) number of those competing and the absolute number of seats reserved. 'There is no mechanical formula by which it can be determined that this opportunity is "equal" between individuals' (Ibid.: 407).

This tension is inherent in the two goals of 'compensatory discrimination' and 'equal opportunity'. By definition, compensatory discrimination allows for reservations of positions for designated groups, which have been historically discriminated against, and who, in normal course, would be disadvantaged in gaining access to a preferred position. However, as soon as the position is reserved, it is not available for non-beneficiaries. That is indeed the meaning of reservation. Does this violate equal opportunity for the general population? If the answer is yes, then the discussion over percentages is redundant and no quotas should be allowed. However, then the stigmatized or historically discriminated groups would not gain access, which was the logic for reservation in the first place. The 1952 case of *Abdul Latif v. State of Bihar* illustrates this tension. Here the issue was the distribution of licences to set up an excise shop, which added another twist in this conundrum. In a case like this, the definition of percentages is even more complicated, as there is no fixed total number of shops from which a certain percentage can be reserved. Each shop which is given to an SC–ST member represents 100 per cent reservation, if the base is taken as one shop. However, if the base is taken as all shops, then the percentage of the quota will be drastically different. Is it possible for the state to count, in advance, the total number of shops which will be set up (over how many years?) and then grant x per cent of these to SCs–STs? This illustrates the fundamental problems in formulating and implementing a percentage rule.

Finally, each reserved position is, by design, denied to all persons who are not eligible for reservation. However, in the end, the case for reservation does not rest on the welfare of those to whom the position is denied, but on the overall advancement of social or national interests. Thus, any discussion on the validity of reservations or any preferential scheme has to rest on an assessment of the impact of the preferences on the advance of the stigmatized groups, and, therefore, on overall social or national impact.

## Designation of Beneficiaries

Quotas for SCs and STs are constitutionally sanctioned and may not be challenged in court. However, as Chapter 2 highlights, constitutionally, caste is not, in itself, a permissible criterion for discrimination. The Indian Constitution seeks to establish a society that is egalitarian, casteless, and classless. This would mean a society where untouchability has been abolished and caste has been rejected as a retrograde institution. Evidence presented earlier shows that the reality is very different. Covert and overt instances of untouchability continue and there is clear evidence of discrimination against Dalits and Adivasis, which strengthens the case for AA in favour of these groups.

For Other Backward Classes (OBCs), though, the issue is more complicated. The Mandal Commission Report (MCR), the National Commission for Backward Classes (NCBC), and the Supreme Court have suggested a set of 'neutral' (that is, not related to caste) criteria: poverty, place of habitation, occupation, and income level, which should be used to determine backwardness, rather than caste. But it is important to recognize that the criteria do not end up remaining completely 'neutral', that is, caste-free, for two reasons. One, since these get examined for each of the OBCs, there is an implicit belief that these markers of dis-advantage need to be seen along caste or community lines, so caste does get included. The other reason these can never be caste-free is that all these so-called neu-tral attributes are actually very closely related to caste status. Thus, even though, for certain jatis, there would be significant *within-caste* inequality, there is sufficient *between-caste* inequality in each of these attributes to believe that these are distributed by caste.

The announcement of the OBC quota at the central-government level revived the old debate over whether caste should be an indicator of backwardness, or whether other criteria should be used. There is a fairly prevalent belief that reservations should be class-based, or based on economic criteria, for two reasons. First, if the state accepts caste as the basis for backwardness, it legitimizes the caste system that contradicts secular principles. Second, the traditional caste system (the jajmani system) has broken down and contractual relationships have emerged between individuals (see Desai 1984). Thus, the argument goes, the life chances of an individual in contemporary India are determined by his/her economic condition and not by membership of any social group. Thus, this position argues that a poor Brahmin and a poor Mahar (a Dalit caste in Maharashtra) will have similar social and economic outcomes that will be in contrast to a rich Brahmin and a rich Mahar. Based on data from Gujarat, Shah (1985) demolishes the latter argument and demonstrates how the objective conditions of different castes are indeed disparate. For instance, controlling for landholding, there is wide diversity in educational attainment by caste.

Prompted by the concern that caste-based policies enhance caste-consciousness, there is a view that one could design 'caste-blind' policies, which under the garb of neutrality will actually end up targeting the same caste groups which are targeted under caste-based AA. This argument is analogous to the race-blind AA argument discussed elsewhere, most notably in France and the US. The way these policies would work would be by designing a set of eligibility criteria, not based on caste, which would be characteristic of a large enough proportion of the target group. Suppose, for instance, that 80 per cent of Dalit families had a monthly per capita consumption expenditure (MPCE) of less than Rs 100. In that case, designing a benefit for all families with MPCE less than Rs 100 will ensure that 80 per cent of the Dalit families are eligible, in addition all non-Dalit families who have MPCE below this threshold. The idea is to find an eligibility criterion which would make a large proportion of the target group population eligible. Darity et al. (2011) demonstrate that a shift from group-based to class-based AA will necessarily dilute the access of targeted groups to AA, no matter how the eligibility criteria are defined. Thus, if for instance, Mahars face systematic exclusion on account of their untouchable status, AA policies will need to target the group, and not the poor across all castes in general. Also, as the previous chapter demonstrated for Karnataka, the announcement of the so-called 'caste-blind' criteria led to a situation where the dominant groups in the state cornered the quota seats.

The Rajasthan state government introduced a proposal to extend quotas for poor upper castes, and in doing so, extend the set of communities which were eligible for AA. The Rajasthan Reservation Bill, 2008, extended the spread of quotas by granting 5 per cent quotas in jobs to Gujjars and 14 per cent to economically weaker section among the forward castes. Interestingly, this did not provoke any seriously adverse media/public reaction, in sharp contrast to the hysterically violent reaction to the announcement of OBC reservations, when an extension of quotas was seen as a deliberate lowering of merit. The implicit assumption underlying this differential reaction could be that poor upper castes are intrinsically meritorious, just backward due to adverse circumstances. It is instructive to note that none of the usual rhetoric about pampering/vote-bank politics accompanied this announcement either.

As mentioned earlier, there are some who are opposed to AA in any form and towards any target group. There is another more nuanced position which opposes caste-based AA but claims to be in favour of AA based on economic criteria, or needs-based AA. Often this opinion overlaps with the view that AA in higher education is too little, too late. In others words, there is a section which favours AA at earlier levels, which is not caste-based. It will be useful to review the experience of the Delhi government, which starting with academic year 2007–8 introduced quotas in schools (primary to Class XII) for children of 'economically weaker sections' (EWS), defined as those whose parental income is less than Rs 100,000 per year from all sources and who have been staying in Delhi for the past five years. Interestingly, these quotas are applicable not only to government-run schools but also to all private schools which run on government-allotted land. Under these provisions, all such schools are supposed to provide free seats, not less than 20 per cent of all seats, to students from the EWS category. In other words, children from lower middle-class families get the opportunity to study in expensive, elite schools, which would have been completely out of their reach earlier. The reaction to these admissions revealed not only the ugly class bias of Delhi's elite, but more important and shockingly, the elitist class bias of private school managements and teachers. Parents of EWS children continue to face hurdles in the admission process (http://www.hindustantimes.com/India-news/NewDelhi/EWS-parents-face-admission-hurdle/Article1-791258.aspx, accessed on 25 August 2012). Actually the situation is much worse as schools make it very clear that EWS families are unwelcome and parents have alleged that they have had forms thrown in their faces, or have been turned away from school premises (http://www.firstpost.com/delhi/schools-throw-the-form-in-my-face-ews-applicant-208108.html, accessed on 25 August 2012). This has now been extended to the entire country as a part of the central government's Right to Education Act of 2011 and the reaction in private schools elsewhere is very similar to what is witnessed in Delhi. A Bengaluru school reportedly cut tufts of hair from EWS students to make their identification easy. These students are made to sit at the back of the class, their lunch boxes are checked, and no homework is given to them (http://www.hindustantimes.com/India-news/Bangalore/Bangalore-school-snips-hair-of-RTE-quota-students/Article1-891101.aspx, accessed on 25 August 2012). Thus, it is not true that when quotas are given on purely economic criteria, or as early educational intervention, they are naturally welcomed as fair. What the opposition to EWS reveals is the fierce and unconditional opposition to the sharing of privilege.

There is the additional argument that caste matters only in rural areas. In urban areas, the argument goes, due to the possible anonymity and the prevalence of modern, industrial, and service-sector contractual relations, labour market outcomes will not be affected by caste affiliations. Indeed, the belief that caste should not matter in urban labour markets is perfectly legitimate. However, Chapter 1 summarizes some key evidence which busts this myth. To reiterate the points made earlier, contemporary occupational distribution indicates that while several jatis, including Dalits, may have moved away from traditional occupations, Dalits tend to be overwhelmingly concentrated in the lower end of the modern occupational spectrum. Additionally, studies confirm the presence of both wage and job discrimination in the private sector, which employs a large part of the industrial workforce and which is free from the purview of AA.

On the whole, evidence suggests that caste remains an important indicator of backwardness in the present. However, for OBCs, since the varna–jati link is more fluid, and because they did not suffer historical discrimination in the form of untouchability, and also since sections of the OBC community are fairly prosperous (the dominant castes or the creamy layer), the caste criterion could be combined with an income ceiling, as it is currently done, so that the truly disadvantaged within the community gain from reservations.

## Is AA by the State Permissible Outside Sections 15(5) and 16(4)?

This leads to the larger question of what kind of AA might be optimal. For instance, should it be quota or non-quota based? If it is quota-based in educational institutions, should qualifying marks be lowered to accommodate beneficiaries (see Pinto 1999 and Srikanth 2000)? The current position is that for admission to most courses, qualifying marks for SC–ST students are lower. While this is done in order to increase the presence of SC–ST students, the long-run merit of this move could be questioned in view of the fact that these students tend not to be able to cope and hence drop out before the course is over. This could be potentially avoided by special assistance during the course such as remedial teaching programmes, but these exist in very few institutions, most notably in the Indian Institutes of Technology (IITs) and in some university departments, but their reach can and should be expanded.

## AA in the Private Sector

Another implication of the last question is whether AA should cover only government institutions or should it extend to the private sector as well. In the wake of liberalization and privatization of the Indian economy, this is an increasingly pressing question. The one sphere where Dalits could hope to find respectable employment is shedding jobs as liberalization puts pressure on government budgets. The growth rate of organized sector employment has been declining between 1997 and 2007. This has happened mainly due to a decline in employment in the public sector. Globalization is creating enormous opportunities for the Indian economy, all of which fall in the private sector. According to the *Economic Survey* of the Ministry of Finance (2009–10: 275), employment in establishments covered by the Employment Market Information System of the Ministry of Labour grew at 1.20 per cent per annum during 1983–94, but decelerated to -0.03 per cent per annum during 1994–2007, and this decline was mainly due to a decline in public sector establishments from 1.53 per cent in the earlier period to -0.57 per cent in the later period, whereas the private sector showed acceleration in the pace of growth in employment from 0.44 to 1.3 per cent per annum.

High growth rates in corporate India have opened opportunities of the kind rarely seen before and it is common knowledge that big money is to be made here. The public sector is often seen as a backwater of inefficiency and students, who can manage it, flock to the high-technology sector. However, neither the private sector, nor the new fully private educational institutions are inclined to implement quotas. Thus, if AA remains confined to Articles 15(5) and 16(4), then steady privatization can, and has, eroded AA significantly.

The Prime Minister of India, Manmohan Singh, set the ball rolling on this question in 2007 by asking if and how AA could be introduced in the private sector. This was followed by another bout of intense public criticism of AA in the media and by the intellectual class and a restatement of all the ills that AA is supposed to have brought in its wake. In response, the Confederation of Indian Industries (CII) and the Associated Chamber of Commerce (ASSOCHAM) drafted a set of policies, more as a part of a package of measures designed to ensure 'corporate social responsibility', rather than specifically to implement any kind of AA (defined as specific policies designed to increase representation of under-represented groups).

One of the main questions which arose at the time was 'how do we know that Dalits are under-represented in the private sector, or more generally, what their actual representation is?' Since data on caste membership of employees is related only to the needs of the existing AA programme, there is no information on caste membership in sectors where there is no AA. In March 2007, the Department of Industrial Policy and Promotion wrote to India's three main industrial organizations requesting data on fresh Dalit recruitments made. Apart from CII, the letter was sent to FICCI (Federation of Indian Chamber of Commerce and Industry), which represents about 443 chambers, associations, and member bodies, and ASSOCHAM, with 300 regional chambers covering 250,000 members from every segment of business since 1920.

Several companies and important individuals in the private sector responded favourably to this and agreed to collect information on the caste composition of their workforce. However, the results of this exercise are not publicly available. We will report the figures from a recent manpower survey conducted by CII. This is not a census of all firms but a survey, so actual figures might vary from the ones reported. This survey finds that in 2010, for instance, on an average 24 per cent of the employees of the surveyed firms in the eastern region (Bihar, Orissa, Chhattisgarh, West Bengal, and Jharkhand) were SCs–STs, with the proportion of SC–ST employees being the highest for blue collar workers. This proportion was higher than that for the northern (Delhi, Haryana, Punjab, Himachal Pradesh, Uttar Pradesh, Uttarakhand, Rajasthan, and Chandigarh) and southern (Karnataka, Andhra Pradesh, Kerala, and Tamil Nadu) regions. Proportions from other regions were similar. According to this survey, in the eastern region, the presence of SCs–STs in senior management of consultancy firms was 3 per cent. Thus, even the limited data point to clear exclusion or under-representation of Dalits in the private sector. However, only 1 per cent of the surveyed firms in the eastern region keep data on ethnic composition of the workforce. Of the remaining, 93 per cent feel there is no need to keep this data and 6 per cent feel that it would be good to have the data. There is no reason to believe that more data will *reverse* this picture. Here we see a classic Catch-22 situation: such measures cannot be implemented until there is data on the social and demographic composition of the employees. And, such data will not be collected for fear of exacerbating caste feelings.

In conclusion, we see that Dalit support for AA in both higher education and jobs is unanimous and overwhelming, against the backdrop of discriminatory tendencies and their relative handicaps. At the same time, many (though hardly all) join several of their general category counterparts in arguing that either reservations should be more targeted (towards poor and rural Dalits, rather than second or third generation recipients of quota admissions, who are viewed as an internal 'creamy layer') or that reservations should be coupled with generous financial aid. The search for the 'truly disadvantaged' continues in India (as it does in all countries with affirmative action), with complex political agendas in the mix.

# 5

# Assessment of the Affirmative Action Programme

Gujaratis know the value of efficiency. They know
how to do business and they always mean business.
And they think the Government should also run like
a business where merit is appreciated. Appointments
and promotions cannot be a matter of charity.

—Shankarbhai Patel, leader of the Akhil Gujarati Vali
Mahamandal, an anti-reservation outfit, 1985

In every country with affirmative action (AA), the
opposition to it in principle is essentially based on the
idea of meritocracy, with the implicit belief that labour
markets and other social institutions reward merit and
efficiency, if allowed to function without hindrance in
the form of AA. There is extensive literature on the

international debate on AA and no summary will be attempted here, except to emphasize the following point. Cross-national comparisons in Darity and Deshpande (2003) reveal that, first, in the presence of discrimination, labour markets do not function efficiently. Indeed, there are strong discriminatory losses in earnings among subaltern groups.

Second, while nowhere in the world has AA proven to be sufficient to close the gaps between the privileged and oppressed groups, there is enough evidence to suggest that the gaps would be larger in its absence (see Darity and Deshpande 2003). A good example is India's northern neighbour, Nepal, the world's only 'Hindu' state until the Maoists captured power in 2008 and established a republic, ending 239 years of royal rule. Its caste composition is dominated by Brahmins and Kshatriyas (Bahun and Chhetris); the number of castes is much smaller than in India. Nepal abolished caste-based discrimination formally in 1963, but had no system of AA and thus, despite the growth of civil society organizations since the 1990s, many 'hierarchical institutions, especially powerful informal networks, behavioural norms, and expectations remained unchanged' (Bennet 2005: 7).

Though they comprise over 20 per cent of Nepal's population, Dalits possessed only 1 per cent of the country's wealth in 2005 (CHRGJ 2005: 8). Collectively Dalits represent 80 per cent of the 'ultra-poor' in Nepal and are highly vulnerable to exploitation. Together they own just 1 per cent of arable land, while only 3 per cent of Dalits own more than a hectare of land. Unlike in India, labour market data are available by caste and the disparity in the occupational distribution is striking. In 2004, Dalits in the rural areas were basically extremely poor, subsistence farmers, and in the urban areas were concentrated at the lowest end of the ladder. There was virtually no Dalit middle class in existence. Interestingly, because Nepal's government is the country's largest employer, discrimination at the workplace directly indicts the government. This suggests that while AA may not be the ideal remedy, its absence, that is, letting labour markets function without hindrance, does not correct for exclusion either. This should not be surprising any more, given the evidence on discrimination presented in earlier chapters.

For a programme which has been extremely contentious, and marked by extensive litigation and protests, there are surprisingly few rigorous empirical assessments of its impact. All the standard anti-AA arguments have been invoked in the Indian context as well, but with virtually no empirical backing. Before listing the arguments, we should note that arguments against OBC reservations are not the same as those against SC–ST reservations, though there is considerable overlap in the two sets of arguments. The difference between the approach to OBC quotas and SC–ST quotas arises primarily because of the assessment about the nature and extent of deprivation and marginalization of the two groups, in that the case for SC–ST reservation is stronger than that for OBCs. Thus, a support for the SC–ST quota might not naturally translate into support for the extension of reservation towards OBCs, where an argument for a more nuanced approach can be (and has been) made (see Deshpande and Yadav 2006).

## Matters of Merit

The most common criticism of AA measures is that they go against the consideration of merit and efficiency by allowing candidates access to preferred positions in higher education and public sector jobs, where they would not have otherwise gained access. The latter part of this statement is obvious—quotas are meant precisely for that. The first part of the statement can actually be verified empirically, and indeed many such empirical studies exist in the context of the US. However, till recently, there was a surprising dearth of detailed empirical studies and the debate proceeded more on the basis of preconceived beliefs, rather than on the basis of hard evidence.

It should be noted as a general point, though, that the discussion on merit is conducted as if merit is a neutral, objective characteristic, independent of the standard used to measure it, similar to height or weight or the number of teeth. The reality is that 'merit' is extremely hard to measure in a standardized way and examination results, while widely used as a proxy for merit, are often not good measures of true underlying ability or talent. Nussbaum (2012: 81) points out how the US debate over race and intelligence quotient (IQ), 'if it has achieved nothing else, has at least made virtually everyone aware that even a test that purports to be a neutral measure of intelligence is full of pitfalls for the child of a minority or immigrant culture or of a less than stimulating home environment.'

145

Exam scores are seen as a relatively non-controversial instrument for allocating scarce seats in institutions of higher education, for providing a cut-off mark. But whether every percentage difference in exam scores reflects a qualitative difference in 'merit' is a moot point: is someone who gets 85 per cent in annual, standard examinations, which encourage learning by rote and formulaic answers, necessarily more meritorious than another person who scores 80 per cent? Maybe or maybe not. The argument is *not* that intrinsic differences in quality do not exist, but that examination scores might not be the best way to gauge them. On a personal note, as a teacher in Delhi University, I see that each successive batch of my students enters with higher qualifying grades than the earlier batch. The escalation in students' entry grades over a decade is striking (over 10 percentage points at least); yet, it is difficult for me to claim that the present batches of students are visibly brighter than the batches I taught 10 years back.

Of course, it can be argued, and has been, that *within* a given cohort of students, the distribution of scores gives a good enough indication of the underlying distribution of merit. Again, subject to some caveats, this would be valid for broad differences in grades (say, 80 per cent versus 60 per cent), but it is not immediately obvious what magnitude of gap between grades signals 'real' or 'true' differences in underlying quality. Just as it is argued that caste-based quotas are an imprecise or rough measure to target 'true' deprivation, exam scores could be seen as an imprecise or rough measure of the underlying 'merit'. It would be useful to recall the experiment on teacher biases in testing reported in Chapter 1 (Hanna and Linden 2009). Nussbaum (2012) gives an example of other kinds of possible tester errors: a question in the examination was as follows: 'Emperor' is the name of: (a) a symphony, (b) a concerto, (c) an aria, (d) a quartet. The testers graded (b) as correct, based on the name of Beethoven's famous concerto, and marked (d) as incorrect, since they were unaware of Haydn's, less famous, Opus 76 Emperor quartet (Nussbaum 2012: 81–2). Such questions require highly specialized and localized cultural knowledge and have very little to do with intelligence and unfortunately, far too many examinations, especially the standardized ones, contain questions of this type.

Finally, what is missed in the debate over lower entry scores for SC–ST students is the value addition that takes place due to being admitted to a prestigious institution of learning. The focus on drop-outs of quota students detracts from the success stories—those who are successfully able to complete the programme. Bowen and Bok (1998) document the long-term positive impact of AA on the lives of beneficiaries who successfully graduate from elite universities in the US, even if they do so with grades lower than their white counterparts. For successful blacks, the transformation in their life chances because of AA is tremendous and the benefits go beyond the final grade they obtained at graduation.

## Quotas Limited in Scope

The second common criticism of the AA programmes is that they have not been able to confer widespread benefits to members of target groups. This is partly due to design: they institute preferences at the level of higher education and prestigious public sector jobs, which are scarce and extremely coveted, but most members of the target groups do not possess the minimum qualifications to access these jobs. The other reason that the benefits are not widespread is because of clustering or cornering of benefits from those in the community who are already advantaged. More generally, as discussed earlier, AA is seen to *promote* casteism and to bestow privileges on certain groups, which are denied to the rest of the population. Again, this is inverting the logic of the AA programme: it is designed to provide access to privileged positions to marginalized groups, which would, in the absence of the programme, not have access to these positions.

All these questions demand careful scrutiny and detailed assessment. Before the more rigorous empirical studies came into existence, Galanter (1984) had undertaken a rough but comprehensive assessment of the AA programme. His main conclusions can be summarized as follows:

- The programme has shown substantial redistributive effects in that access to education and jobs is spread wider in the caste spectrum than earlier, although redistribution is not spread evenly throughout the beneficiary groups. There is evidence of clustering, but Galanter believes that these reflect structural factors, since the better situated enjoy a disproportionate share of the benefits in any government programme, not just in AA programmes.

- The vast majority of Dalits are not directly affected by AA, but reserved jobs bring a manifold increase in the number of families liberated from subservient roles.

- In the short run, beneficiaries might get singled out and experience social rejection in offices, college hostels, and other set-ups where they are introduced through AA. However, in the long run, education and jobs weaken the stigmatizing association of Dalits with ignorance and incompetence. Moreover, 'resentment of preferences may magnify hostility to these groups, but rejection of them exists independently of affirmative action programmes' (p. 549).

- Reserved seats do provide representation to SCs–STs in legislative bodies, but that may not get reflected in enhanced, targeted policies towards these groups for several reasons. One, these candidates are elected by a common electorate and, hence, SC–ST candidates have to appeal to a wider, multi-group electoral constituency, and tailor programmes accordingly. Two, these candidates typically belong to political parties which have a larger agenda than that of Dalit empowerment, which their elected representatives, including Dalits, have to reflect upon.

- AA has kept the beneficiary groups and their problems visible to the educated public, but it has not motivated widespread concern for their inclusion beyond what is mandated by government policy.

Thus, Galanter concludes that AA has been a partial but costly success. It has accelerated the growth of a middle class and SC–ST members have been brought into central roles considered unimaginable a few decades ago. However, even this crude calculation will not work for assessing OBC reservations because, first, OBC quota is much more recent and, two, OBCs are not stigmatized in the same way as SCs, because their traditional occupations do not put them in humiliating and subservient roles in the same way as they do SCs. Thus, OBC reservations have to be assessed very differently from SC–ST reservations.

Corbridge (2000) gathered a wealth of quantitative and qualitative data over the 1980s and 1990s from the Jharkhand region of south Bihar in order to assess the impact of reservations on the tribals of that region.

He found that the reservation system had benefited mainly the tribal elite, which had formed over the 1940s and 1950s via jobs in the mines, who were mostly men and residing in urban areas. However, the capture of reserved jobs by middle-class STs was not so pervasive that less affluent tribals have no hope of landing a reserved job. In fact, in his study, almost half the jobs available seemed to be going to less affluent tribal men (and some women). Many of them were earlier rural residents who had subsequently moved to the city and had benefited from AA during their college years. Thus, poorer but well-educated tribals were relatively more represented in Class II jobs (rather than in Class IV) jobs. Also, he found that it is 'not only members of a pre-existing tribal elite who are using state patronage for their own ends, nor are these ends entirely private' (p. 65). The reservation system had served to expand the size of the tribal middle class. It had also forced government officers to pay more than lip-service to the idea of AA, in that they had to institute a roster system of job advertisements, where each job came with a serial number and an indication of whether it was reserved for a particular community. The existence of reservations served to enhance tribals' consciousness about their rights and about asking for compensation from the authorities. Since this study was conducted before the formation of Jharkhand state, Corbridge argues that the strengthening of tribal identity would also help the movement for the formation of a separate state.

## Empirical Assessments of AA

Lately, particularly with the announcement of the OBC quota in higher education in 2006, there have been a spate of interventions by economists, some to question the legitimacy of quotas, most to question AA altogether (see Somanathan 2006 and Sundaram 2007). However, it is interesting that none of these contributions are based on an actual empirical assessment of specific data related to the implementation of AA. Thus, until Deshpande and Weisskopf's (2011) study, there was not a single empirical assessment of the impact of AA on jobs in India. A monetary cost–benefit evaluation of job quotas is not possible because of the manner in which the Indian programme is formulated. Quotas have existed since independence (actually even longer), so there is no 'before-and-after' data to examine the changes in productivity of an enterprise as a result of preferential hiring.

## Productivity Impact of AA

In an attempt to empirically study the effects of AA in the labour market, Deshpande and Weisskopf (2011) chose to focus on Indian Railways to assess if AA, that is, the presence of SC–ST employees who have gained entry through quotas, had impacted productivity negatively. The study covered the period 1980 to 2002 for eight of the nine railway zones in existence during the period and used a variety of econometric techniques to examine the impact of AA on total output and on total factor productivity. The broad results are discussed here.

Analysing an extensive data set on the operations of one of the largest employers in the public sector in India, the Indian Railways, the study found no evidence to support the claim of critics of AA that increasing the proportion of SC and ST employees will adversely impact productivity or productivity growth. On the contrary, some of the results of the analysis suggest that the proportion of SC and ST employees in the upper

(A+B) job categories was positively associated with productivity and productivity growth.

The finding of such positive associations in the case of A and B jobs is especially relevant to debates about the effects of AA on behalf of members of SC and ST communities for two reasons. First, the impact of AA on productivity is likely to be much more affected by the efficacy with which high-level managerial and decision-making jobs are carried out than the efficacy with which lower-level, semi-skilled, and unskilled jobs are fulfilled. Thus, critics of reservations are likely to be, and indeed are, much more concerned about the potentially adverse effects of reservations at the highest decision-making levels than at the lower levels. Second, it is precisely in A and B jobs—far more than in C and D jobs—that the proportions of SC–ST employees would not have risen had it not been for quotas. Indeed, reservations have been indispensable for raising the proportion of SC–ST employees. Even without reservations, one would expect substantial numbers of SC–ST applicants to be hired for C and D jobs, especially for D category cleaning staff; but without reservations, very few SC–ST applicants would have been able to attain jobs at the A and B levels.

While the focus of the study was on measuring productivity and its link with the proportion of employees who were SCs–STs, the paper also examined some other issues. For instance, critics of AA have alleged that the frequency of Indian Railways' accidents is likely to be linked to quotas because reservation policies result in a larger proportion of less competent railway officials and lower overall staff morale (see, *Indian Express*, 19 September 1990). Railway accidents are obviously an important indicator of poor railway performance; they generate adverse consequences that go far beyond the loss of damaged equipment and the failure to complete a planned passenger or freight trip. The study, therefore, thought it useful to see if trends in Indian Railways accident rates could be related in any way to trends in SC–ST labour proportions.

Correlating the all-India yearly railway accident rate (the total number of accidents per million train kilometres) over the period of the study (1980–2002) with the corresponding all-India figures for the proportion of SC–ST employees in total employment, the study found correlation coefficients of -0.69 for all employees and -0.93 for employees in the upper-level A and B categories (GoI, Ministry of Railways, *Annual Statistical*

*Statements*). The second, higher correlation is the most relevant, both because Indian Railways employees serving in management and professional positions are especially responsible for guarding against accidents and because the data on SC–ST employees in the C and D categories fail to count many SC–ST employees who do not declare themselves as such. It should be noted that this correlation is *negative*, not positive as critics of AA would expect.

The finding of a highly significant negative correlation between the all–India accident rate and the SC–ST proportion of A+B category employment results from the fact that the former has been declining and the latter rising (both fairly steadily) over the last few decades. This is strong evidence that higher SC–ST employment proportions are not resulting in higher accident rates—unless, of course, there are other likely determinants of the accident rate that have also shown steady trends (and the appropriate sign) over the same period. The most plausible alternative explanations for decreasing accident rates are increasing electrification of signals, improvement in track quality, and safer track crossings (including better-guarded level crossings and more bridges over tracks). There is indeed evidence of positive time trends in each of these alternative determinants (see Ministry of Railways 2005–6, esp. pp. 18–25). There is insufficiently detailed data, however, to include such variables in more complex estimation techniques such as a multivariate regression analysis of accident rates. While such an analysis might well counter the notion that higher SC–ST employment proportions actually promote greater safety, it seems unlikely that it could undermine the conclusion that higher SC–ST employment proportions do no harm.

The results of this analysis of productivity in Indian Railways are consistent with the results from productivity studies in the US, in that there is no statistically significant evidence that AA in the labour market has an adverse effect on productivity. The results of this study are stronger, however, in that the study does find some suggestive evidence that AA in the labour market actually has a favourable effect—in particular, that the growing proportion of SC–ST employees hired at the high-level A and B category railway jobs, largely through India's reservation policies, has contributed to greater overall railway productivity.

It was beyond the scope of this study to explain just how and why AA in the labour market may have such a favourable effect. However, the answer may be found in one or more of the following suggestions that others have advanced to explain such a finding. Individuals from marginalized groups may well display especially high levels of work motivation when they succeed in attaining decision-making and managerial positions because of the fact that they have reached these positions in the face of claims that they are not sufficiently capable—in consequence of which they may have a strong desire to prove their detractors wrong. Or individuals from marginalized groups may simply believe that they have to work doubly hard to prove that they are just as good as their peers. Having greater numbers of SC–ST managers and professionals working in high-level A+B positions in the Indian Railways might also serve to increase productivity because their community backgrounds make them more effective in supervising and motivating SC–ST workers in C and D jobs. This recalls the arguments in favour of AA in US educational institutions made to the Supreme Court by US military officers, who want to avoid having just white men in charge of troops that are disproportionately of colour (see Weisskopf 2004: Preface). Finally, improvements in organizational productivity may well result from a greater diversity of perspectives and talents made possible by the integration of members of previously marginalized groups into high-level decision-making teams. Page (2007) shows convincingly how groups that display a wide range of perspectives outperform groups of like-minded experts.

## Assessing AA in Higher Education

Weisskopf (2004) provides a comprehensive comparison of AA policies in the US and in India. A substantial part of this discussion is focused on AA policies in Indian universities. From his evidence, as well as from other studies reported in this chapter, it is clear that a large majority of SC–ST candidates owe their presence in institutions of higher education to reservation policies. In other words, these students would not be receiving higher education, if it were not for AA policies. While empirical studies on effects of AA in higher education are very few due to lack of data, the few studies that exist point towards the fact that SC–ST students find it hard to succeed in competitive entrance examinations due to past handicaps (lack of good quality schooling, lack of access to special tutorial or coaching centres that prepare candidates for open competitive examinations, and so forth).

Evidence presented in Weisskopf (2004) suggests that at least half the seats reserved for SCs and at least two-thirds of the seats reserved for STs remain unfilled, if all institutions of higher education are considered together. He argues that this is because of 'wastage' (dropping out) as well as 'stagnation' (repeating courses because of failure or attendance gaps) at prior levels of education. While these are very serious problems, the real pity is that a mechanical approach to the issue of AA means that no effort is made to understand the basic underlying factors that cause drop-outs and stagnation (which are discrimination and deprivation and lack of access to good-quality education at prior levels), and thus no serious efforts are made to remedy them. Since the overwhelming opinion remains anti-AA, the larger the proportion of drop-outs, the more it 'proves' the contention of the anti-AA opinion—that quotas are costly and useless. As a matter of fact, there are specific remedial measures that can be applied to address these problems such as bridge courses, special courses in mathematics and English (the two areas with the maximum gaps between SCs and 'Others'), and summer courses. The University Grants Commission, a government body designed to regulate higher education, has special funds allocated for these courses, but these funds remain unutilized for the most part, both because of lack of awareness about these sources of funds and, more seriously, because of a lack of serious will to make the AA programme succeed. Given that there is no monitoring and no penalties for lackadaisical implementation, institutions, even those at the feet of the central government, can turn a blind eye to the issue of unfilled quota seats.

Desai and Kulkarni (2008) examine AA in higher education by focusing on outcomes, that is, by examining the question of whether educational inequalities between SCs and STs, on the one hand, and upper caste Hindus, on the other hand, have reduced, by using data from successive NSS rounds between 1983 and 2000. They calculate 'transition probabilities' across six levels of education (probability of making a transition from primary to middle school, from middle to high school, and so forth). Their study is rich in its detail and its bottom line is clear. Educational inequalities between SCs–STs, on the one hand, and upper-caste Hindus, on the other hand, have significantly declined over time, particularly at the primary education stage. For the middle and high school levels, there is a decline too, but it is not significant. At the college level, the inequalities between ST men and upper-caste Hindus have declined, but for ST women, SC men, and SC women, inequalities have increased. They attribute the declines to AA. This is suggested by the fact that a similar decline is not seen for Muslims, who do not get any preferential treatment. The authors suggest that the decline in inequalities at the primary level might be due to AA in employment. However, in college education, where AA is directly applicable, they find that inequalities have actually widened, which puts a question mark on the efficacy of AA. Also, they find that after accounting for income and residence, SCs experience greater disadvantage in college education than STs.

The reasons for AA in higher education not being able to successfully narrow the gaps is a cause for concern, but as stated earlier, the gaps would, in all likelihood, have been even larger in the absence of AA. The issue of higher drop-out rates for reserved category students is often discussed and this is attributed to the fact that they are placed in programmes for which they are not well-suited: the 'mismatch hypothesis'.

So far, there have been only three substantive quantitative studies which gauge the impact of AA in higher education by focusing on the mismatch hypothesis: that AA actually harms targeted students by placing them in programmes for which they are academically unsuited. Thus, there is a mismatch between the academic preparedness of the students and the scholastic demands of the college. The first study, by Bertrand et al. (2008), focused on individuals applying to an engineering college, via a competitive entrance examination, in one Indian state in 1996. Engineering colleges are among the most prestigious educational institutions in India. The authors first took a census of all students applying to this engineering college and found that the qualifying scores for admission were roughly 480/900 for upper-caste individuals, 419 for OBCs, and 182 for SCs. These score disparities provide elementary support for the hypothesis that lower-caste students would not be able to perform in colleges and will not benefit from AA because of the mismatch between their basic skill levels and the skill requirements of engineering education (*the mismatch hypothesis*). This could lead to wastage and drop-outs. To better understand the outcomes across caste groups, the authors then interviewed about 700 households from the census of all applicants between 2004 and 2006 (approximately 8–10 years after the entrance examination). They surveyed both the applicants and their parents to gauge life outcomes including income and occupation, job satisfaction, social networks, and caste identity.

Their first finding was that contrary to popular belief, caste-based targeting did result in the targeting of individuals who were more economically disadvantaged—the parental income of upper-caste students displaced by AA was Rs 14,088, compared to Rs 8,340 among displacing lower-caste students. Similarly, 41 per cent of the displaced students came from a household in which the head held at least a master's degree, compared to only 14 per cent of the displacing students; 59 per cent of the displaced students had attended an English private school, compared to only 35 per cent displacing students.

Their second finding was about labour market outcomes. They found that despite much lower basic skills (as measured by scores in the entrance exam), those who were admitted through AA benefitted economically from attending the engineering college. Depending on the specifications, attending the engineering college increased lower-caste members' monthly income between Rs 3,700 and Rs 6,200. This corresponds to an increase of 40 to 70 per cent. In other words, *they found no evidence of the mismatch hypothesis*. In addition to improving earning potential, they found that AA could also increase access to more satisfying careers, measured in terms of job quality and satisfaction. These two findings (of higher earnings and better job quality) resonate with the findings contained in Bowen and Bok's (1998) seminal study of long-term benefits of AA in the context of US.

However, they also found evidence of the 'creamy layer' as well as gender imbalance within those who benefitted from AA, much like the Corbridge study. Specifically, they found that those from higher socio-economic backgrounds, and men more than women, within the lower-caste groups benefitted more. Finally, they also tested for AA's effect on applicant attitudes and, somewhat surprisingly, found that upper-caste students displaced by AA did not end up with more negative attitudes towards lower castes or towards AA in general. However, lower-caste students who benefitted from AA programmes ended up being stronger supporters of AA.

The second empirical study of the mismatch hypothesis is by Bagde et al. (2011), which analysed data from 214 engineering colleges in one state in India. They had data on student performance in the entrance examination as well as in the high school completion examination. All students were admitted through a common entrance test and the admission rules were clear and transparent. Colleges had discretion in admissions up to 20 per cent of their available seats. The remaining 80 per cent seats were filled through the common admission system; 50 per cent seats were reserved for students belonging to 6 different castes in pre-decided proportions. Most of these colleges were affiliated to one university, which set a common syllabus for all students and administered a common examination, which made a comparison of academic performance easy. The way in which the admission system worked in their sample of colleges was: priority for admission to these engineering colleges was based on a candidate's rank in the entrance examination and on the caste and gender of the candidate. Thus, the highest-ranked individual in a caste could choose any college. Then, the second highest chose a college. This process continued as long as the college had a seat available for the caste and gender of the applicant. Scores in the high-school leaving examinations and in entrance tests reflected a gradation based on caste: average scores of STs were the worst, with those of SCs being the next, followed by 'backward castes' and finally, the best scores were obtained by general category students.

A big benefit of quotas is that they provide access to students from disadvantaged castes to colleges and courses to which they would have had no access in the absence of affirmative action. This study found both these to be significant: AA increased college attendance with effects that were proportionately the greatest for members of the most disadvantaged castes. Similarly, they found that improved priority in college selection improved achievements (measured by scores on a comprehensive examination administered after the first year of the programme), with proportionately greater effects among the more disadvantaged castes. Finally, they found that for all castes, an increase in priority for college choice resulted in improved academic performance in college—thus, they found no evidence of a mismatch—that is, quotas *harming* intended beneficiaries. They also discuss a counterfactual scenario, without AA, in which members of disadvantaged castes would have attended colleges with weaker peers (given that their entrance examination scores would be lower). These colleges would presumably have faculty which would be academically less able. In which case, the positive effect of college selection on academic achievement, which the study found, might not be seen.

The third study, which is the most recent one (Robles and Krishna 2012), contrary to these findings, suggests that in highly technical courses, there is mismatch and that Dalits do not catch up with the non-Dalit students in terms of grades—in other words, they start with lower grades and graduate with lower grades. However, the study found that AA targets the population it is designed for: targeted students are poorer than the average displaced students. Given the larger benefits associated with AA, even if there is a gap in the graduating grades between SCs and non-SCs, if the targeting is accurate, then admission to prestigious courses would alter the lives of those who get in through AA.

## Impact of Political Reservations

There is a great deal of evidence from several countries which shows that since social identity (caste, gender, and so forth) tends to be strongly correlated with socio-economic status, citizens with the same social identity tend to have similar policy preferences. Pande (2003) takes this as the starting point of her study, and argues that for reasons for equity and efficiency, policies which are in the interest of marginalized groups need to be implemented, and this provides the prima facie reason for improving the representation of these groups in decision-making bodies, given that traditionally these would be under-represented. She examines if reservations in state legislatures for disadvantaged groups increases their political influence. She finds that political reservations increase targeted transfers (such as targeted welfare expenditure in the state plan) towards groups that are targeted by reservations. Thus, reservation for SCs and STs does provide them with policy influence.

Similar conclusions at the village level are seen from the study by Besley et al. (2004), where the availability of public goods for SC–ST households increases significantly if the constituency is reserved (for SCs–STs), compared to non-reserved constituencies. Through a variety of estimation techniques, they establish that the enhanced targeting comes from reservations.

Chattopadhyay and Duflo (2004) studied the consequences of mandated representation for women in gram panchayats (GPs) by conducting a detailed survey of all investments in local public goods in a sample of villages in two districts, Birbhum in West Bengal and Udaipur in Rajasthan, and compared investments made in reserved and unreserved GPs. They found that reservations affect policy decisions in that women's preferences are better represented. In West Bengal, they found that women complained more often than men about drinking water and roads and thus, there was greater investment in these two services in GPs reserved for women. In Rajasthan, women complained more often than men about drinking water but less often about roads, and thus there were more investments in water and fewer investments in roads in GPs reserved for women. They also examined if the nature of public goods provisions can be attributed to the gender of the *Pradhan*, rather than to other consequences of reserving seats. They found that it was the gender of the Pradhan (and not the other characteristics of women Pradhans—that they were less educated, from poorer backgrounds, and had less experience than male Pradhans), which explained this impact and thus confirmed a result seen more widely—that the gender of the elected representative does influence policy decisions. This provides strong empirical support to the logic which led to political reservations in the first place.

Patnaik (2005) examined the impact of reservations, both for SCs–STs and women, on participation and accountability in four panchayats in Odisha. He examined participation by focusing on attendance in regular GP meetings; participation in setting the agenda; raising issues in meetings; and involvement in decision-making processes such as taking decisions in planning, budgeting, location of developmental projects, and selection of beneficiaries in the panchayats. He found that members of marginalized groups recorded lower rates of participation measured by all these criteria, primarily because of social restrictions, economic compulsions, and household work. For women members, restrictions on mobility for upper-caste women were imposed mainly by their husbands or family members, whereas Dalit women faced restrictions both on account of their caste and gender, even though the restrictions on their mobility were fewer. Household work and distance to the panchayat office were two reasons which impeded the participation of women in panchayats. On the whole, he found that panchayat members from reserved groups were still impeded by strong structural barriers, which had kept them marginalized for generations, and this prevented their effective participation in panchayats.

While Patnaik's conclusions, prima facie, might seem at variance with those of the other studies, it is useful to remember that the studies are not strictly comparable in terms of the central question they seek to answer and the methodology that they use. The earlier studies examined policy outcomes, whereas the latter study looked at the process which led to the outcomes. Of course, the two are linked and thus, the latter ought to be seen more appropriately as highlighting some of the challenges inherent in translating reservations into empowerment, which naturally would be a longer, more difficult process and this study underscores some of the problems. The former set of studies indicate that despite challenges, significant gains in terms of a shift in policy focus have already been seen.

Jaffrelot (2003), in discussing the political rise of low castes in north India, highlights some tensions inherent in what he terms the 'silent revolution'—the transfer of power, peacefully, from upper caste elites to various subaltern groups. While his analysis is mainly about OBCs, the issues he raises have a broader applicability and the constraints faced by the OBCs would be faced even more strongly by the Dalits, given their traditional subordinate position. First, he argues that such a transfer of power, in other contexts, would be accompanied by violence. The reason this is by and large peaceful in India, violent episodes notwithstanding (such as during the Mandal agitation), is due to the fact that the transfer is incremental. To a large extent, upper castes still hold the reins of power and OBCs (and in some cases Dalits) form the second rung of leadership. Given the educational and social backwardness of the latter two, they will not be able to dislodge the upper castes for a long time. He also points out the tremendous unevenness in the rise of low-caste politicians—in Uttar Pradesh and Bihar, one sees a much more pronounced rise than in Rajasthan, for instance. Also, the conflict or the transfer of power is not clear-cut; most political parties are not organized solely on upper-caste or lower-caste lines—all, including the Dalit-dominated Bahujan Samaj Party (BSP), have upper-caste members. He also suggests that liberalization of the economy has opened up new arenas and opportunities for upper castes, more lucrative than government jobs, and thus, they might not regret their traditional hold over the bureaucracy being challenged. In Deshpande (2011), I discuss the issue of the impact of liberalization on inter-caste disparities briefly, and suggest that contrary to wishful thinking, the new opportunities opened up by liberalization might not be available to Dalits to the extent needed to close disparities. In particular, they do not as yet have the skills needed to take advantage of the new kinds of jobs which are getting opened up due to liberalization and globalization. Finally, Jaffrelot (2003) suggests that the rise of the lower castes is not linear and irreversible. There is no clear-cut unity among lower-caste parties or individuals, made more complicated by the fact that OBCs and SCs are often at odds, given their conflicting class interests (witness the antagonism between the BSP and the Samajwadi Party in Uttar Pradesh). In addition, there is a great deal of intra-Dalit rivalry and conflict—Mahars and Chambhars in Maharashtra; Jatavs and Bhangis in Uttar Pradesh; or Yadavs and Kurmis.

Keeping this larger picture in mind helps us understand a critical reality about political reservations: that they will help increase representation and access of traditionally marginalized groups such as low castes and women. However, the translation of this increased representation into real power is bound to be a long journey, which will traverse an uneven, non-linear, and rocky road. However, the existence of the challenges should not be seen as proof of the futility of reservations; instead, collectively we need to focus on how to minimize the challenges.

# 6

# Quotas and Beyond

Given the nature of India's affirmative action (AA) policy, quotas are naturally more relevant in urban areas, even though their existence allows the possibility for rural educated Dalits to aspire to formal-sector government jobs. However, not all rural Dalits might be interested in this avenue for their livelihoods. They, more often than not, might neither have the opportunity nor the desire to secure the education levels necessary to obtain jobs via quotas. Thus, if economic and social marginalization of Dalits is to be countered, other measures in rural areas have to be as much on the agenda as the quotas are. Noteworthy among these are land reforms and rapid generation of non-farm employment, especially in the small-scale manufacturing sector. The Chinese experience demonstrates the tremendous potential of both these measures—land reforms during the 1949 to 1978 era and rural industrialization, via township and village enterprises (TVEs)—in transforming the lives of the rural peasantry, especially the landless agricultural wage labourers. In a large, labour abundant, predominantly rural economy such as India, the importance of these measures cannot be overstated. If the existence of a quota system is regarded as the beginning and end of the AA programme, large sections of the rural poor, majority of whom are Dalits, will continue to remain marginalized.

In any event, if we limit the discussion to quotas, given the significant marginalization of other communities (for example, Muslims) as well as the demands of other marginalized sections to be included in the ambit of reservations, it could be argued that the Indian policy is reaching the limits of a quota-based approach to counter discrimination and exclusion, even if the 50 per cent rule is relaxed. As our earlier discussion suggests, quotas have been successful in enabling the creation of a Dalit middle class, which is an important marker of positive or enabling inclusion, and in liberating several families from the tyranny of traditional stigmatizing and oppressive jobs. However, there is a large section of Dalits which is untouched by quotas in government-provided jobs and education. Thus, quotas might be one instrument, but should not be regarded as a universal panacea for caste-based discrimination.

## The Diversity Index

Given the multiplicity of fissures and axes of disadvantage, it would not be out of place to suggest that India should address caste disparity but not at the cost of ignoring other, very pressing, dimensions of group divisions. Contemporary India offers plenty of examples of how a state of persistent exclusion generates resentment and hostility that manifests itself in violent, secessionist forms. The urgency of increasing diversity in a variety of spheres cannot be overemphasized. The Sachar Committee Report, accordingly, recommended that concrete steps should be taken to increase diversity in public spaces. Accordingly, the Ministry of Minority Affairs (2008) appointed an expert group to create a Diversity Index (DI) to measure diversity in public spaces, with a focus on education, employment, and housing.

179

Here is how the Diversity Index is conceptualized. To begin with, DI should measure the gap between the proportion of the group (say, Muslims, or women, or Dalits) in an institution and its proportion among the 'eligible population'. Thus, for a bachelor's degree course, all those who have passed high school constitute the eligible population. This gap is then calculated as a proportion of the share of the group in the population. The gap could be positive (for over-represented groups) or negative. The DI only takes into account negative gaps, since the idea is to quantify under-representation. There are three broad dimensions across which DI is calculated separately: caste, religion, and gender, and the different numbers are integrated *horizontally* (across the three social categories of caste, religion, and gender, using semi-flexible weights, reflecting the needs of the institution) and *vertically* (across the different tiers in an institution, say categories of employees like managerial and clerical, if one were to calculate DI for the workforce, or categories of students like undergraduate, postgraduate, and diploma, if one were to calculate DI for students) to yield one single number that is a composite measure of diversity in that institution. The detailed methodology is explained in the report of the Ministry of Minority Affairs (2008).

The next step is classifying institutions (whether public or private) according to whether they have low (DI value between 0 and 1/3), medium (between 1/3 or 2/3), or high (between 2/3 and 1) diversity and repeat this exercise every five years, tied to the cycle of plan allocations by the government.

The idea is to transform this system into action across all institutions in the country, both public and private, by linking the DI of an institution with financial rewards/penalties such that the exercise of measuring diversity becomes a part of the social ethos. With this aim, the expert group proposed the creation of a Diversity Commission at the national level, an autonomous body answerable to the executive. This body (and its corresponding lower level institutions) will have the basic task of evaluating, ranking, and publicizing the status of institutions annually in a Diversity Report. In addition to financial incentives/ penalties, publicizing the status of institutions via this report would provide yet another source of rewards/ disincentives to the extent that institutions value their public reputation.

The proposed DI system has several advantages: it is transparent, includes the major social groups, allows institutions flexibility in choosing weights to be applied to the social groups, is applicable across the board, and makes the target institutions stakeholders in the system by creating a system of financial rewards. It is not rigid and mechanical. However, when this proposal will be operationalized, if at all, is best known to the powers that be.

## Rethinking AA as a 'Quotas Plus' Policy

An examination of the link between inter-caste disparity and state-level differences in state domestic product (SDP) (as an indicator of how rich the state is) indicates that neither higher growth nor high SDP level alone reduces/eliminates inter-caste disparity (Deshpande 2011). Thus, especially given the compelling evidence, targeted policies to eliminate caste disparity are needed. In other words, AA in India is essential and, in fact, needs stronger implementation. However, in order to increase its efficacy, it has to be less mechanical: provision of quotas should be seen as the beginning of AA, not its end, as is the current practice. A big problem with the AA programme is that there is no monitoring done and, indeed, there are no penalties for evading AA. Thus, the mere announcement of quotas is seen as sufficient, and very little attention is paid to outcomes: how many seats get filled, if there are unfilled seats, what might be the problem, what happens after a beneficiary gets in—all very critical questions that hardly receive any consideration by the government. Further, just providing entry into jobs or educational institutions is not sufficient. There have to be supplementary measures that need to be mandatorily incorporated: remedial teaching, counselling, and other measures to lower the incidence of drop-outs; skill enhancing programmes; and so forth, which will ensure that the benefits of entry into prestigious jobs and educational programmes are fully utilized. To be effective, AA should contain self-liquidating and self-perpetuating features: as AA becomes stronger at the entry level, it should be gradually lowered at the later stages. But for this, strict monitoring of outcomes, with penalties for non-compliance is essential. Indeed, Ambedkar himself envisaged quotas as a temporary measure designed to create a level playing field, after which they would no longer be needed. He believed that with proper implementation, quotas would be redundant in 10 years.

As with AA programmes the world over, the Indian programme is bitterly opposed by non-beneficiaries both on meritocratic arguments as well as on grounds of non/inadequate performance, elitism, promoting casteism, and so forth. Each of these issues has been discussed and it has been suggested that, first, labour markets in the real world do not function on the basis of first-best, perfectly competitive principles, but are, in fact, discriminatory to the detriment of the marginalized groups. Second, the Indian programme is only partially successful and perhaps flawed in several ways (for example, too mechanical, no monitoring, no penalties for non-implementation, no provisions for self-liquidating features), but in the absence of an alternative, comprehensive, and clearly articulated alternative (such as *arguably* the diversity index), it should be continued. The idea of abolishing quotas can meaningfully be mooted only after they have been implemented in their entirety and have been in place for at least a decade (to follow Ambedkar's original timeline).

Third, there is no evidence in support of the claim that AA lowers productivity or efficiency. As for the charge that AA programmes promote casteism (or racism in other contexts) that they are designed to counter, this is a highly insidious and fallacious argument, also not unique to the Indian context. The utterly erroneous assumption this argument makes is that there is no casteism in the absence of AA programmes. If this were true, the material reality of the low castes would be the opposite of what it is at present and AA would be redundant.

It is worth reiterating the point which was made in the introduction. Quotas or preferences are simply means to provide access to privileged positions in society. Preferential policies of any kind, whether quota-based or not, do not touch the basic issue of disparity in wealth distribution. As the Indian economy is privatizing, restricting AA to government jobs and education in India will gradually make it redundant, so it must be extended to the private sector. For it to be meaningful, AA should be applicable to the entire economy (for example, as in the US or Malaysia). Also, while even the suggestion of AA in the private sector is still to take hold in the corporate sector, there seems to be an uncritical acceptance of hereditary reservations in business houses in India.

Finally, 'outside the box' measures must be considered that go beyond the scope of the current AA programme: free, compulsory, and good quality primary education, provision of basic health facilities, adequate nutrition, vigorous expansion of non-farm employment, land reforms wherever feasible, subsidies/support for Dalit business/self-employment, and establishing a strong anti-discriminatory framework. Given that scavengers are the most stigmatized of all Dalit communities, an elimination of the degrading practice of manual scavenging, coupled with the building of latrines will not only provide the basis for de-stigmatizing a large community, but will also provide significant health benefits. All these measures will benefit a much larger section of Dalits than the current AA programme. The important thing to note is that the existing AA programme and these supplementary measures need not be considered mutually exclusive. They can strengthen and reinforce each other. What is needed is a strong political will to end caste discrimination and reduce caste disparities. Admittedly, there would be costs to all these measures, but the benefits of integrating large sections of the nearly 160 million Dalits, unleashing the suppressed reservoir of talent is the need of the hour for the rapidly growing Indian economy.

# Appendix

## NCBC Guidelines for Inclusion in
## the Central List of OBCs

The commission, after studying the criteria/indicators
framed by the Mandal Commission and the commissions
set up in the past by different state governments and other
relevant materials, formulated the following guidelines for
considering requests for inclusion in the list of Other
Backward Classes:

## A. Social

1.  Castes and communities, generally considered as socially
    backward.
2.  (a) Castes and communities, which mainly depend
        on agricultural and/or other manual labour for

their livelihood and are lacking any significant resource base.

(b) Castes and communities, which, for their livelihood, mainly depend on agricultural and/or other manual labour for wage and are lacking any significant base.

(c) Castes and communities, the women of which, as a general practice, are for their family's livelihood, engaged in agricultural and/or other manual labour, for wage.

(d) Castes and communities, the children of which, as a general practice, are, for family's livelihood or for supplementing family's low income, mainly engaged in agricultural and/or manual labour.

(e) Castes and communities, which in terms of caste system, are identified with traditional crafts or traditional or hereditary occupations considered to be lowly or undignified.

(f) Castes and communities, which in terms of the caste system, are identified with traditional or hereditary occupations considered to be 'unclean' or stigmatised.

(g) Nomadic and semi-nomadic castes and communities.

(h) Denotified or Vimukta Jati castes and communities.

*Explanation*: The term refers to castes/communities which had been categorised as Criminal Tribes under the Criminal Tribes Act, 1924, Act No. VI of 1924, passed by the Indian Legislature and repealed by the Criminal Tribes (Repeal) Act, 1952, Act No. XXIV of 1952 and subsequently referred to as Denotified or Vimukta Jatis.

3. Castes and communities, having no representation or poor representation in the State Legislative Assembly and/or district-level Panchayati Raj Institutions during the ten years preceding the date of the application.

*Explanation*: This is only intended to measure, as an indicator, the presence of a caste or community in these bodies.

The term 'poor representation' may be taken to refer to a caste or community whose presence in the body is less than 25% of its proportion in the population.

## B. Educational

1. Castes and communities, whose literacy rate is at least 8% less than the State or district average.

2. Castes and communities of which the proportion of matriculates is at least 20% less than the State or district average.

3. Castes and communities, of which the proportion of graduates is at least 20% less than the State or district average.

## C. Economic

1. Castes and communities, a significant proportion of whose members reside only in Kachha houses.
2. Castes and communities, the share of whose members in number of cases and in extent of agricultural lands surrendered under the Agricultural Land Ceiling Act of the State, is nil or significantly low.
3. Castes and communities, the share of whose members in State Government posts and services of Groups A & B/Classes I & II, is not equal to the population-equivalent proportion of the caste/community.

## D. Illustration

Population-equivalent proportion

| | |
|---|---|
| Population of a State | 10,00,000 |
| Population of the caste/community under consideration in the State | 1,00,000 |
| Proportion of the population of the caste/community under consideration to the total population of the State | 10% |

Number of posts in Class-I in the State           1,000

Therefore, population equivalent proportion
of Class-I posts in the State in respect of the
caste/community under consideration        100

*Explanation-1*: In the case illustrated above, if members belonging to the caste/community under consideration hold 100 Class-1 posts or more, its share is equal to or more than its population-equivalent proportion.

In that case that caste/community will not be considered to have fulfilled this indicator of backwardness.

In the case illustrated above, if the members of the caste/community under consideration have 99 Class-1 posts or less, its share is less than its population-equivalent proportion and will, therefore, be considered to have fulfilled this criterion of backwardness.

*Explanation-2*: This guideline is only an indicator to assess backwardness or its absence and has no relation to the condition of inadequacy under Article 16(4).

*Explanation-3*: The population-equivalent proportion of posts may be composed of posts secured through merit only or through reservation only or through both—figures need to be furnished separately for posts secured through merit/posts secured through both—figures need to be furnished separately for posts secured through merit/posts secured through reservation.

In addition to the above, arising from Article 16(4) the following conditions have also to be fulfilled: Castes and communities, which are not/are inadequately represented in the Central Government posts & services of Group A & B, each Group/Class should be taken separately.

## Procedural Clarification on Guidelines

1. The above social, educational and economic guidelines for consideration of requests for inclusion in the list of Other Backward Classes are intended to aid the Bench/ Commission to identify castes and communities which deserve to be included in the list of OBC in terms of the National Commission for Backward Classes Act and not to fetter due exercise of discretion by it.

2. The term 'local', wherever used, is intended to mean State level or intra-State regional level or district level, as appropriate, in the light of the demographic distribution of the caste/community concerned.

   However, wherever the Bench/Commission has adequate reasons, the sub-district level positions may be taken into account.

   In some guidelines, State or local, or State or district have been given as alternatives. In such instances the appropriate alternative may be chosen depending on the circumstances such as demographic distribution, ready availability of data etc.

3. Some of the guidelines are capable of quantification but data are not available in every State. In respect of States, where such data are readily available (e.g. specific percentage figures), the Bench/Commission may examine the cases before it in terms of such quantifiable data and their own observations as well and other relevant materials that may be available to it. In respect of States where such quantifiable data are not available, the Bench/Commission may consider castes/communities on the basis of their own observations and other relevant materials that may be available to it.

4. Under each of the categories A, B & C, of guidelines, there are 3 or 4 guidelines. They are not necessarily cumulative. Cumulative data would no doubt be advantageous. But where data-base does not readily permit, each caste or community may be considered in terms of such of the guidelines under each of the categories A, B & C as are practicable.

5. Regarding the condition at D, till information regarding the position of each caste in the Government of India's services becomes readily available, it may be presumed that this factor is fulfilled by a caste/community/sub-caste/synonym/sub-entry, in case it is found that it fulfills the guideline in C 3.

6. Wherever a caste or community fulfills the guidelines 2(e) or (f) or (g) or (h), the Bench/Commission may take it as adequate evidence of backwardness. In such cases, the Bench shall take into account such other data/information that may be made available to it or comes to its notice, and it may make such further inquiry as it deems proper and necessary. Having done so and being satisfied that there are no sufficient grounds to take a contrary view regarding the backwardness of the caste or community making the request, the Bench may, after examining the matter of inadequacy of representation as indicated in D, proceed to formulate its findings.

7. Occupations mentioned at guideline 2(e) and 2(f) may include traditional artisanal crafts; fishing, hunting, bird-snaring; agricultural labour on the lands of others; earth work, stone-breaking, salt manufacturing, lime-burning; toddy-tapping; animal rearing; butchery; hair-cutting; washing of clothes; ferrying by boat; safai (i.e. 'scavenging'); knife grinding, grain roasting; entertaining through song and dance, acrobatics jugglery, snake-charming, acting; begging or mendicancy.

*Explanation*: This refers only to castes or communities which traditionally depended on begging or mendicancy in the past i.e. until it was prohibited by law.

The Bench/Commission may take into account any other occupation which may be similar to these occupations.

8. In respect of any case of request, found to be one of apparent 'clerical' error, or factual mistakes at the stage of preparation of the common lists and if there is no contrary view expressed and data furnished before or otherwise available to/in the notice of the Bench/ Commission such castes/communities may be included and findings/advice formulated to that effect.

9. In case of synonyms/sub-castes/different names of the same caste or community/local variants of the same caste or community, if and after it is established that, they are, in fact, such synonyms/sub-castes/different names of the same caste/local variants, etc. and if there are no contrary views expressed and data furnished before or otherwise available to/in the notice of the Bench/ Commission and the Bench/Commission does not find any ground to take a contrary view, such synonyms/ sub-castes/different names of the same caste/local vari-ants of the same caste, such cases may be included, and findings/advice formulated to that effect.

10. In all cases, publicity regarding the date and venue of the sitting of the Commission's Bench and the castes/ communities etc. to which the sitting pertains may be made through mass media and all those who have any

views to express or data to furnish to the Bench may be invited to do so, in addition to addressing the State Governments and applicants to furnish all material and data in their possession.

11. These guidelines of identification and procedure will be applicable to all categories of States/UTs and all categories of castes/communities whether included in the State list but in the Mandal list or included in the Mandal list but not in the State list, or included in neither.

# References

Abraham, Vinoj. 2012. 'Wages and Earnings of Marginalized Social and Religious Groups in India: Data Sources, Scope, Limitations and Suggestions', Mimeo.

Ambedkar, Bhim Rao. 1936. *The Annihilation of Caste*. Jallandar: Bheem Patrika Publications.

———. 1945. *What Congress and Gandhi Have Done to the Untouchables*. Bombay: Thacker and Co. Ltd.

Bagde, Surendrakumar, Dennis Epple, and Lowell J. Taylor. 2011. 'Dismantling the Legacy of Caste: Affirmative Action in Higher Education', Mimeo.

Bayly, Susan. 1999. 'Introduction' to *Caste, Society and Politics in India from the Eighteenth Century to the Modern Age*. Cambridge: Cambridge University Press.

Bennet, Lynn. 2005. 'Gender, Caste and Social Exclusion in Nepal: Following the Policy Process from Analysis to Action', Working Paper for the World Bank Conference on 'New Frontiers of Social Policy:

Development in a Globalising World', 12–15 December. Available at http://siteresources.worldbank.org/INTRANETSOCIALDEVELOPMENT/Resources/Bennett.rev.pdf, accessed on 10 February 2010.

Bertrand, Marianne and Sendhil Mullainathan. 2003. 'Are Emily and Greg More Employable than Lakisha and Jamal? A Field Experiment on Labour Market Discrimination', National Bureau of Economic Research Working Paper No. 9873.

Bertrand, Marianne, Rema Hanna, and Sendhil Mullainathan. 2008. 'Affirmative Action in Education: Evidence from Engineering College Admissions in India', National Bureau of Economic Research Working Paper No. 13926.

Besley, Timothy, Rohini Pande, Lupin Rahman, and Vijayendra Rao. 2004. 'The Politics of Public Good Provision: Evidence from Indian Local Governments', *Journal of the European Economic Association*, 2(2–3): 416–26.

Bowen, William G. and Derek Bok. 1998. *The Shape of the River: Long Term Consequences of Considering Race in College and University Admissions*. Princeton, NJ: Princeton University Press.

Census of India. 1931. Census Commissioner, Government of India Central Publication Branch.

Center for Human Rights and Global Justice (CHRGJ). 2005. 'The Missing Piece of the Puzzle: Caste Discrimination and the Conflict in Nepal', Report by CHRGJ, NYU School of Law.

Chakravarti, Uma. 1987. *The Social Dimensions of Early Buddhism*. New Delhi: Oxford University Press.

Chattopadhyay, Raghabendra and Esther Duflo. 2004. 'Women as Policy Makers: Evidence from a Randomised Policy Experiment in India', *Econometrica*, 72(5): 1409–43.

Corbridge, Stuart. 2000. 'Competing Inequalities: The Scheduled Tribes and the Reservation System in India's Jharkhand', *Journal of Asian Studies*, 59(1): 62–85.

Darity, William Jr. and Ashwini Deshpande (eds). 2003. *Boundaries of Clan and Color: Transnational Comparisons of Inter Group Disparity*. London: Routledge.

Darity, William Jr., Ashwini Deshpande, and Thomas E. Weisskopf. 2011. 'Who is Eligible? Should Affirmative Action be Group- or Class-based?', *American Journal of Economics and Sociology*, 70(1): 238–68.

Desai, I.P. 1984. 'Should "Caste" Be the Basis for Recognising Backwardness', *Economic and Political Weekly*, 19(28): 1106–16.

Desai, Sonalde and Veena Kulkarni. 2008. 'Changing Educational Disparities in India in the Context of Affirmative Action', *Demography*, 45(2): 245–70.

Deshpande, Ashwini. 2011. *The Grammar of Caste: Economic Discrimination in Contemporary India*. New Delhi: Oxford University Press.

———. 2012. 'Deprivation, Caste Inequality and the Maoist Conflict in India', in N. Jayaram (ed.), *For Satish*

*Saberwal: Essays in Historical and Comparative Studies.* New Delhi: Orient Blackswan.

Deshpande, Ashwini and Katherine Newman. 2007. 'Where the Path Leads: The Role of Caste in Post University Employment Expectations', *Economic and Political Weekly*, 42(41): 4133–40.

Deshpande, Ashwini and Thomas E. Weisskopf. 2011. 'Do Reservation Policies Affect Productivity in the Indian Railways', Centre for Development Economics Working Paper No. 185, May.

Deshpande, Satish and Yogendra Yadav. 2006. 'Redesigning Affirmative Action: Castes and Benefits in Higher Education', *Economic and Political Weekly*, 41(24): 2419–24.

Deshpande, Satish and Mary John. 2010. 'The Politics of Not Counting Caste', *Economic and Political Weekly*, 45(25): 39–42.

Dirks, Nicholas. 2002. *Castes of Mind: Colonialism and the Making of Modern India.* New Delhi: Permanent Black.

Dushkin, Lelah. 1979. 'Backward Class Benefits and Social Class in India 1920–1970', *Economic and Political Weekly*, 14(14): 661–7.

Galanter, Marc. 1984. *Competing Equalities: Law and the Backward Classes in India.* New Delhi: Oxford University Press.

Guhan, S. 2001. 'Comprehending Equalities', in S. Subramanian (ed.), *India's Development Experience.* New Delhi: Oxford University Press.

Hanna, Rema and Leigh Linden. 2009. 'Measuring Discrimination in Education', National Bureau of Economic Research Working Paper No. 15057.

Human Rights Watch (HRW). 1999. *Broken People: Caste Violence against India's Untouchables*. New York, Washington, London, Brussels: HRW.

Jaffrelot, Christophe. 2003. *India's Silent Revolution: The Rise of the Low Castes in North Indian Politics*. New Delhi: Permanent Black.

Jaiswal, Suvira. 2000 [1998]. *Caste: Origin, Function and Dimensions of Change*. New Delhi, Manohar.

Jodhka, Surinder and Katherine Newman. 2007. 'In the Name of Globalisation', *Economic and Political Weekly*, 42(41): 4125–32.

Kannabiran, Kalpana. 2012. *Tools of Justice: Non-discrimination and the Indian Constitution*. New Delhi: Routledge.

Liddle, Joanna and Rama Joshi. 1986. *Daughters of Independence: Gender, Caste, and Class in India*. New Delhi: Kali for Women; London: Zed Books; Totowa, NJ: US Distributor, Biblio Distribution Center.

Madheswaran, S. and Paul Attewell. 2007. 'Caste Discrimination in the Indian Urban Labour Market: Evidence from National Sample Survey', *Economic and Political Weekly*, 42(41): 4146–53.

Ministry of Finance. 2009. *Economic Survey 2009–10*. New Delhi: Oxford University Press.

Ministry of Minority Affairs. 2008. *Report of the Expert Group on Diversity Index.* New Delhi: Government of India. Available at http://www.minorityaffairs.gov.in/sites/upload_files/moma/files/pdfs/di_expgrp.pdf, accessed on 14 April 2012.

Ministry of Railways. 2005–6. *2005–06 Yearbook.* New Delhi: Government of India.

Nambissan, Geetha B. 2010. 'Exclusion and Discrimination in Schools: Experiences of Dalit Children', in Sukhadeo Thorat and Katherine S. Newman (eds), *Blocked by Caste: Economic Discrimination in Modern India.* New Delhi: Oxford University Press, pp. 253–86.

Navsarjan Trust. 2010. *Understanding Untouchability: A Comprehensive Study of Practices and Conditions in 1589 Villages.* Ahmedabad: Robert F. Kennedy Centre for Justice and Human Rights and Navsarjan Trust.

Nussbaum, Martha. 2012. 'Affirmative Action and the Goals of Education', in Zoya Hasan and Martha C. Nussbaum (eds), *Equalizing Access: Affirmative Action in Higher Education in India, United States, and South Africa.* New Delhi: Oxford University Press, pp. 71–88.

Page, Scott. 2007. *The Difference: How the Power of Diversity Creates Better Groups, Firms, Schools, and Societies.* Princeton: Princeton University Press.

Pande, Rohini. 2003. 'Can Mandated Political Representation Provide Disadvantaged Minorities Policy Influence?

Theory and Evidence from India', *American Economic Review* 93(4): 1132–51.

Pandian, M.S.S. 2007. *Brahmin and Non-Brahmin: Genealogies of the Tamil Political Present.* New Delhi: Permanent Black.

Parikh, Sunita. 1997. *The Politics of Preference: Democratic Institutions and Affirmative Action in the United States and India.* Ann Arbor, Michigan: The University of Michigan Press.

Patnaik, Pratyusna. 2005. 'Affirmative Action and Representation of Weaker Sections: Participation and Accountability in Orissa's Panchayats', *Economic and Political Weekly*, 40(44/45): 4753–61.

Pinto, Ambrose. 1999. 'Saffronisation of Affirmative Action', *Economic and Political Weekly*, 34(52): 3642–5.

Prakash, Shri. 1997. 'Reservation Policy for Other Backward Classes: Problem and Perspectives', in V.A. Pai Panandiker (ed.), *The Politics of Backwardness: Reservation Policy in India.* New Delhi: Konark Publishers, pp. 29–87.

Robles, Veronica, C. Frisancho, and Kala Krishna. 2012. 'Affirmative Action in Higher Education in India: Targeting, Catch Up and Mismatch', NBER Working Paper No. 17727.

Rodrigues, Valerian (ed.). 2002. *The Essential Writings of B.R. Ambedkar.* New Delhi: Oxford India Paperbacks.

Royster, Deirdre. 2003. *Race and the Invisible Hand: How White Networks Exclude Black Men from Blue-collar Jobs.* Berkeley: University of California Press.

Sachar Committee Report. 2006. *Social, Economic and Educational Status of the Muslim Community in India.* New Delhi: Government of India. Available at http://minorityaffairs.gov.in/sites/upload_files/moma/files/pdfs/sachar_comm.pdf, accessed on 23 January 2012.

Sachchinananda. 1997. 'Reservation and After: The Case of Bihar', in V.A. Pai Panandiker (ed.), *The Politics of Backwardness: Reservation Policy in India.* New Delhi, Konark Publishers, pp. 161–82.

Sahoo, Niranjan. 2009. *Reservation Policy and Its Implementation across Domains in India: An Analytical Review.* New Delhi: Observer Research Foundation and Academic Foundation.

Shah, Ghanshyam. 1985. 'Caste, Class and Reservation', *Economic and Political Weekly,* 20(3): 132–6.

Shah, Ghanshyam, Harsh Mandar, Sukhadeo Thorat, Satish Deshpande, and Amita Baviskar. 2006. *Untouchability in Rural India.* New Delhi: Sage India.

Sharma, Smriti. 2012. 'Hate Crimes in India: An Economic Analysis of the Violence and Atrocities against Scheduled Castes and Scheduled Tribes', Centre for Development Economics Working Paper No. 213, May.

Sheth, D.L. 2004. 'Caste, Ethnicity and Exclusion in South Asia: The Role of Affirmative Action Policies in Building Inclusive Societies', HDR Regional Background Paper, United Nations, 2004/13.

Siddique, Zahra. 2009. 'Caste Based Discrimination: Evidence and Policy', Institute for the Study of Labour (IZA), Discussion Paper No. 3737. Available at SSRN at http://ssrn.com/abstract=1550883.

Singh, K.S. 1993. *The Scheduled Castes*, National Series: The People of India, Volume 2. New Delhi: Oxford University Press.

Somanathan, Rohini. 2006. 'Assumptions and Arithmetic of Caste Based Reservations', *Economic and Political Weekly*, 41(24): 2436–8.

Srikanth, H. 2000. 'No Shortcuts to Dalit Liberation', *Economic and Political Weekly*, 35(13): 1121–3.

Sundaram, K. 2007. 'Fair Access to Higher Education Re-visited—Some Results for Social and Religious Groups from NSS 61st Round Employment–Unemployment Survey, 2004–05', Centre for Development Economics Working Paper, No. 163.

Thimmaiah, G. 1997. 'Karnataka Government's Reservation Policies for SCs/STs and OBCs', in V.A. Pai Panandiker (ed.), *The Politics of Backwardness: Reservation Policy in India*. New Delhi: Konark Publishers, pp. 108–60.

Thorat, Sukhadeo and Paul Attewell. 2007. 'Legacy of Social Exclusion', *Economic and Political Weekly*, 42(41): 2436–8.

Thorat, Sukhadeo and Katherine S. Newman (eds). 2010. *Blocked by Caste: Economic Discrimination in Modern India*. New Delhi: Oxford University Press.

Vijayan, P.P. 2006. *Reservation Policy and Judicial Activism.* New Delhi: Vedam Books.

Weisskopf, Thomas E. 2004. *Affirmative Action in the United States and India: A Comparative Perspective.* London: Routledge.

Xaxa, Virginius. 2002. 'Ethnography of Reservation in Delhi University', *Economic and Political Weekly*, 37(28): 2849–54.

Zweigenhaft, Richard L. and William G. Domhoff. 1998. *Diversity in the Power Elite: How Women and Minorities Reached the Top.* New Haven: Yale University Press.

# Index